PEACEFUL PASSING

~

Die When You Choose
with
Dignity & Ease

Robert S. Wood

Published by
In Print Publishing
Sedona, AZ
(520) 284-5298 • Fax (520) 284-5283

All Illustrations by the Author

Cover Design & Typesetting:
Pat Sumstine, My Imagination, Sedona, Arizona

Front Cover Photograph: Sky hare
Koji Kitagawa/SuperStock

Wood, Robert S.
    Peaceful passing: die when you choose with dignity and ease / Robert S. Wood. - 1st ed.
    p. cm.
    LCCN: 00-130441
    ISBN: 1-886966-17-6

    1. Death 2. Conduct of life. 3. Death–social aspects. 4. Spiritual life. I. Title.

BD444.W66 2000   155.9'37
                      QBI00-900196

For Deanne
with love

Also by
Robert S. Wood

Desolation Wilderness

Pleasure Packing

Mountain Cabin

Goodbye, Loneliness!

The 2 oz. Backpacker

Whitewater Boatman

Dayhiker

Homeopathy, Medicine That Works!

Have More Fun!

ACKNOWLEDGEMENTS

Thanks first of all to Jerry and Esther Hicks for permission to present the valuable and comforting teachings of Abraham—the heart of this book. I'm also indebted to Cela Coleman, Helen Wysham, Annette Tannascoli and "Gentle Closure" for their contributions to the text.

Editor Biz Burnett turned my scribblings into English and supplied constant, unfailing encouragment along the way. Publisher Tomi Keitlen expertly transformed the raw manuscript into this book—with the help of designer/typesetter, Pat Sumstine.

I'm also grateful to my team of readers: Bonnie Hartenstein, Jan & Charles Lundstrom, David & Joan Steninger, Stafford & Veronica Archer, Bill & Florence Johnson, Carl Felt, my wife Deanne, and David Malcolm, who gave me valued feedback when I needed it.

Without the help of all these good people, this book on easy death might never have come to life.

TABLE OF CONTENTS

The mystery that is death... What readers can expect... A preview of Death in America today...a revolution in the making and why... A brand new option... Now you can change your attitude toward death, passing peacefully when you want... Access tremendous freedom and a happier life...What you'll know by the end of this book.

An example...How my letter to a dying friend helped him choose an easy, prompt, dignified and peaceful passage by simply letting go.

The Right To Die Movement... The experiment in Oregon, Dr. Kevorkian, legality and legislation. The sad state of death in our culture...The fear, conspiracy of secrecy and denial by state, church, science and parents that threaten our Right to Die... Historical highlights... Helpless hospital death, life supports, statistics... The death of hope...Life becomes preparation for aging, illness, death...Suicide and euthanasia... Near Death Experiences... Trends... Changing Attitudes... Hopeful signs... The new option being offered.

The Only Real Authority on Death...because they've been there, done that, innumerable times...What they have to tell us is exciting, consistent, dependable and wise...Taking the mystery out of channeling... Accepting the concepts of immortality, an afterlife, and reincarnation...So suspend your disbelief...What you hear will shrink your fear and fill you with relief.

The Universal View of creation: channeled words of wisdom from the non-physical world, explaining how things really work—starting with the universe and working inward toward the individual and his or her life and death....A highly-structured overview of how the universe functions...and a way to test this thesis.

With thought and emotion, not action. We attract what we get—all of it. Modern science heartily agrees with the experts on the other side. Because we alone create events, we are totally safe from the creations of others, so the need to fear them disappears...There is no luck, chance, fate, accident or coincidence; only random, unconscious creation. So we can take conscious, deliberate control of our lives and our deaths.

Because we create everything that happens to us, we therefore create our deaths. Once we decide to let go of life, we choose the time and circumstances of our death, though usually unconsciously. Death is always a choice...even when it seems to be accident, illness, natural disaster—even murder. Once we decide to die, we begin to attract death. We can then die deliberately and peacefully by simply Letting Go when and how we consciously want. When someone dies, it happens by choice, so there's no need to grieve or mourn for them.

Advice, procedures and techniques from channeled entities for peacefully parting from your body with dignity and re-emerging into the delicious non-physical realm, with ease, joy and enormous relief—deliberately and in full control...Learning how will destroy your fear of death.

How to digest and experiment with these new ideas, revolutionary concepts and exciting possibilities for both life and death... How to apply, adapt, test and integrate the teachings...Summary digest of the principles.

My authority for writing this book as demonstrated by the success and achievement I attribute to applying these teachings...How I consciously, deliberately create a happy, successful, healthy, prosperous life with my intentions, expectations and beliefs...How you can, too...My plans for Letting Go when I'm ready to say goodbye to this lifetime.

True stories of the deaths of four people who refused to wait for a slow painful death to overtake them. Instead they took charge of their quick and dignified departures to pass peacefully and easily, alone and on their own terms.

~

INTRODUCTION

This little book had a sudden and surprising beginning. One day it dawned on me that a number of things I'd recently learned fit neatly together to synergistically produce an exciting new concept of death—a new paradigm. For the first time I saw previously invisible connections.

This new paradigm, I realized, had the power to prevent untold suffering, replace ignorance with knowing, turn negative into positive, change lead into gold. And I felt I could put it all together in a small package that would give new hope for life while demolishing the fear of death.

Here are the elements that suddenly connected: Death is the biggest blank spot on the map of mankind's knowledge. Because none of us have experienced it and lived to tell the tale, we know absolutely nothing about it. Death in our society is truly *terra incognita*. Being essentially unknown, Death makes us feel helpless and frightened. It's probably the greatest single, longest-lasting source of worry in our lives.

Our ignorance and fear of death make us prey to all kinds of terrifying myths about it. In this vacuum of information, the myths have grown more and more grotesque—helped along by self-seeking institutions that use fear of the unknown to enforce control over an innocent populace.

For instance, we've come to believe that death is utterly beyond our control, and that an honorable death in our culture requires physical deterioration—in total disregard for human suffering or the quality of life.

No wonder we go through life with the brakes on, living at half speed, anxiously looking over our shoulder, letting fear erode the quality of our lives. And we accept this misery as normal and inescapable.

So it's ironic that we've always had access to matchless authorities on death and the hereafter, experts with vast experience of innumerable deaths who are willing, even eager, to explicitly tell us what awaits us both in death and the afterlife. And their news is all good. The only hell, they assure us, is on earth—not in the beyond!

These authorities are beings like us who once walked the earth. They speak to us now from the other side through channels. They tell us that we're totally, tragically wrong about death and the afterlife. What we mindlessly dread is actually something to look forward to!

First of all, they tell us, the essential person never dies. All that we've become simply shifts to the non-physical realm. Modern science completely concurs.

The experts further assure us—and all Near Death Experiences on earth validate their view—that every death is a suicide because nobody can die until they make the decision to let go of life. People die because they want to, when they're ready to go!

This revelation leads to the exciting realization that we each have the power to take full control of our passing! We don't have to wait helplessly for death to overtake us—or violently kill the body with suicide or euthanasia. We can each take full control of our dignified death!

At this point I began excitedly digging out every reference I could find from channeled entities on death. I discovered that all we have to do to take complete control of our death is (1) discard our old belief that we're utterly helpless, replacing it with the conviction that we're fully in charge; and (2) make our ultimate decision to let go of life both conscious and deliberate.

I have known for some years that I enjoy complete control of every aspect of my life, that I'm constantly creating with my desire and belief and expectation. Using this knowledge, I've created great success in every area of my life. So it was easy, by extension, to believe that I also enjoy complete control of my death. Death, after all, is merely the final event of life.

I'm far from the first to make this discovery. The experts report that spiritually aware, enlightened people everywhere take control of their deaths by rejecting society's fatalistic, helpless beliefs and replacing them with the knowing that they are totally in control—just as wise men and women have done down the ages.

All we have to do, the experts assure us, is flip a mental switch or two. We have a right to die when and how we want—even young and healthy—and we have the ability to do so at will. It's okay, they tell us, to depart whenever we want.

When it's time to move on, it's only necessary to sink into a deep, final sleep with the clear and passionate intent of waking up in the non-physical realm. Anyone can do it. Advance preparation is not essential, although it helps. Examples in chapters two and eleven show how the process works.

Furthermore, the firsthand picture the experts paint of life in the hereafter is something to look forward to. In fact it's so appealing that I sometimes find I actually envy the dying for the wonderful relief they're about to receive, and for the heavenly—not hellish—fresh adventure that awaits them!

For myself, when that adventure becomes more alluring than remaining in this lifetime, I'll simply release the essential me from my body. That's how I intend to change worlds when I'm ready. You can, too.

The purpose of this book is to show you how. It will also show you how to create a happy, successful remainder of your life. It's all waiting in the pages that follow. Get ready for a genuine journey of discovery!

Robert S. Wood
Sedona, Arizona

"*There is no cure for birth or death
save to enjoy the interval.*"

–GEORGE SANTAYANA

"Do not take life too seriously; you will never get out of it alive."

–ELBERT HUBBARD

1

AN OVERVIEW

This is the happiest little book you'll ever read about death because it offers exciting good news. Like enlightened people worldwide, you can learn to take charge of your peaceful, natural dignified death. You can die without drugs or the stigma of suicide or euthanasia. It's the ultimate solution to life's universal problem: gaining personal control over private natural death. By giving you back full control of your passing, it takes the terror out of dying, restoring peace and freedom to the rest of your life.

How much do we really know about death? Not much. We know it's the end of our physical life, and that's about all. The rest is hope, fear, myth, superstition and wild conjecture. Self-appointed authorities tell us what to believe and how to behave, but they don't know any more than we do. They not only have no experience with dying, they often have ulterior motives. No one here on earth knows what death is really like. To find out, we have to consult those who've actually been there.

We know that each of us has to die. But how? When? Under what circumstances? No wonder death is the biggest, longest-running source of anxiety in our lives. There's no greater, more frightening unknown. Nothing makes us feel more vulnerable and helpless. We can't fully enjoy life because we're busy fearing death. And the control we yearn for is steadfastly denied us by society. We're sentenced to endure unlimited pain, indignity and misery, often at enormous financial cost, without being able to lift a finger in protest. The horror stories are endless.

That's why thoughtful people everywhere are intensely interested in better options for dying. We're all eager for an easy way out, and demand for something better has never been higher. In fact there's a not-so-quiet rebellion underway against the painful, helpless death prescribed by society. Consider the evidence:

Derek Humphry's book *Final Exit*, spent 18 weeks on the New York Times best seller list after a Wall Street Journal article reported that, "it tells you how to kill yourself." The Hemlock Society, spearhead of the Right to Die Movement, has a web page on euthanasia and assisted suicide that gets 70,000 hits per month. Demand for Dr. Kevorkian's services climbs steadily as sympathy grows for his attempts to help the suffering. Polls show three quarters of all Americans now approve legalizing assisted suicide. The first such law was passed in Oregon in 1994, and similar legislation has been introduced in 15 states. No matter what their religion, people are demanding more control over death.

But death in America is getting tougher to control. The suicide rate climbs inexorably, and experts say official numbers are just a fraction of the true total figure. Among the young (ages 15-24), suicide is soaring. A few decades ago, the vast majority of Americans died peacefully at home in their beds. Now, over 80% (and rising) die in nursing homes and hospitals, where ever more sophisticated life support systems prevent them from passing naturally (and where individual control is denied).

Every year, medical science devises more heroic measures for keeping people alive—whether they want to live longer or not. As a result, some 70% of all deaths are somehow "managed or negotiated" as doctors and lawyers conspire to pull the plug on unwanted life support systems for patients no longer competent to convey their desires.

Deadly prescription drugs like barbiturates, are getting harder to obtain. Doctors, afraid of huge malpractice suits, are nervous about prescribing; unskilled at pain management and uncomfortable with patients they can't cure, reflecting that they're backed by a medical hierarchy that callously resists change and reform and steadfastly opposes physician-assisted death.

The church ceaselessly opposes any form of suicide, determined to keep it illegal for anyone to help another person die. Though the Oregon law allowing conservative physician assisted death has functioned well for several years, it's about to be killed by a bill in congress that makes it a severely punished crime to help anyone die. That's why Doctor Kevorkian is in jail and his assistant in exile.

Parliaments in Britain, Canada and Australia have also refused to listen to their electorates' pleas for choice in dying, denying all attempts to legalize assisted death. No wonder people everywhere are rebelling, desperate for help, hungry for a better option. They know the Right to Die is—or should be—what activists and the press call "the ultimate civil liberty." Details will be found in Chapter 3.

This hunger and desperation has loosened rigid attitudes and replaced them with growing curiosity. Prejudice is fast fading against such unfamiliar topics as Out of Body Experiences (OBE's), Near-Death Experiences (NDE's), Past Life Regression, Channeling, Reincarnation, psychics and metaphysics (defined as strong evidence that you just can't see). Raymond Moody's book on life after death *Life After Life* which discusses NDEs and proven communication from the other side, has sold some three million copies. Attitudes are swiftly changing.

Channeled entities seem to be our only real authorities on death and dying...because they've actually been through it. They alone can tell us how to die the easy way, when we're ready, without violence, drugs or assistance. They also describe what it's like on the other side, because that's where they're speaking from. (They say it's a lot like dreaming—without the nightmares—but more vivid than real life, and much more like heaven than hell.) Overall, they paint an appealing and liberating picture of the afterlife.

This little book is the first to offer a simple, natural, non-violent, dignified option for the peaceful self delivery they suggest. But it's not unknown on earth. Far from it. It's been practiced forever, though long forgotten by most societies. Its revival now can revolutionize our attitudes toward death, freeing us from lifelong fear-induced obsession. It's the path of passing chosen by wise men down the ages and increasingly employed today by enlightened, spiritually aware, advanced, thoughtful people everywhere, people who know how the universe works and who choose to live deliberately according to its laws.

Many of them use it to assert full control over their deaths while escaping the culture's punitive laws and grotesque taboos. Now you can learn their secrets. What's offered here is legal, private, safe, easy, drug-free, undetectable and peaceful...the ultimate option for leaving this life. It restores individual control over the time, place and circumstance of your passing.

Being totally free of the stain of suicide and the difficult-to-arrange, often illegal and anxious partnership of assisted death and euthanasia, it avoids the wrath and disgrace of church and society, leaving friends and relatives free of guilt and shame. And it escapes all the pain, misery and indignity of lingering hospital death—and the attendant ruinous costs that often eat up a lifetime of savings.

This book is for people who believe in our absolute right to decide how and when we die. It offers a fresh start, a joyful rebirth, an exciting new beginning, an adventure to look forward to when the appeal of this lifetime finally fades. It involves totally free choice, a premeditated transition to the other side, a deliberate, easy, painless, peaceful exit from a tired and worn out body. You don't have to be sick—or even old. You can leave while the going's good. It's your life, so you have the right to determine when it ends. Just decide to go when you're ready to move on.

Anybody can do it. You simply choose to let go of your body while sleeping, releasing the life force that keeps us all alive. Instead of killing the body, you simply let go of it. Modern science now agrees that we create our whole reality—every event in our lives—with our minds and our emotions, not with our actions. It therefore follows that we determine when we're ready to depart our bodies. That means technically every death is a suicide—even if it seems otherwise.

So why wait for a painful accident to happen (like Princess Di and Dodi)? This book shows you how to die consciously and deliberately, when you want to, rather than unconsciously or when you have to. Just go to sleep intending to wake up on the other side. If your desire or need is great enough, you can make the transition at a moment's notice. No advance preparation is necessary—although it helps.

You can enjoy your life right up to the moment of your departure. Throw a farewell party, or pass away privately, quietly and alone—or choose something in between. You're in complete control. You don't need a doctor or a partner or drugs. There are no prerequisites or qualifications. Your religion and beliefs—if any—don't need to matter.

By the end of this book you'll not only know how to die peacefully and easily when you want, you'll realize that death is not the end. It's only one short step in an eternal cycle in which you shed your worn out body. There's no need to physically kill your body as with suicide and euthanasia. Just release the Life Force the way enlightened people do. With lifelong fear of death diminished, if not demolished, you'll be able to see death as a potential friend—one which will bring you unimaginable relief by instantly wiping out all doubt, fear, guilt, blame, frustrations and inhibitions...even if you're young or healthy.

If you're ill and in pain, the relief is vastly greater. What awaits you, so we're told, is a sudden expansive feeling of well-being that's delightful beyond description. That prospect can marvelously transform your view of death from lifelong fear to something to look forward to when you're weary of this existence.

While learning how to peacefully leave this world and access huge relief, you'll learn how to live easier, happier and more successfully—like the enlightened people who live deliberately and pass on the same way—a magnificent gift for the rest of your life. If this sounds mysterious or too good to be true, an example in the next chapter will make everything clearer.

~

"Come lovely and soothing death."

–WALT WHITMAN

"Death is the cure of all diseases."

–THOMAS BROWNE

2

TOM'S STORY

My wife and I met Tom and Mary on a three week summer hiking trip in the Swiss Alps. They were both in their seventies, churchgoers, active and highly independent. As we walked together daily, we became good friends. Before long we realized we shared something else. Back home in California we both had summer cabins in the mountains— and they happened to be within walking distance of one another!

When we returned home we continued to walk together. Tom and Mary's cabin was in a valley by a river. Ours was a thousand feet above it on a ridge. We often walked down the trail to visit them by the river, then they'd drive us back to our cabin and we'd all have lunch on our deck. Over the years we walked a lot of trails together.

Then one summer Tom told us he was sick. His usual

cheerfulness was replaced by silence and he often seemed tired. Our walks became shorter and Tom had trouble keeping up. Privately, Mary told us it was cancer. By mid-summer Tom couldn't hike anymore, but he drove the three of us to the trailheads, then came back to pick us up, always trying hard to be cheerful.

Sometimes we went out to dinner together, but we didn't talk about Tom's problem. Then one day I found myself alone with Tom in his cabin. Suddenly he turned to me and said, "Bob, I just don't know what to do! The doctors keep changing their stories. They tell me I'll get well, but the drugs keep getting stronger. And I get weaker all the time. I don't know what to do next!" He looked at me intently, waiting—but for what? He was wringing his hands and his knuckles were white. I felt he was asking me for some kind of help, but I didn't know what he wanted. I tried to find out by gently inviting him to tell me, but he couldn't. Maybe he didn't know. When I left I felt badly because I hadn't been able to help.

By the end of summer Tom was in the hospital, sedated for his pain. Mary kept us posted on his condition. She is one of the frankest, strongest women I've ever known. She told me that Tom was miserable at being cooped up and drugged, but the doctors said he was strong and might last a long time. He hated the hospital, hated being indoors, but he didn't need life supports. "I wish he did," Mary said, "Then we could just pull the plug. He's really depressed. I wish he could just let go and die!"

That's when I got the idea for the letter. I told her about that day in the cabin when he had reached out to me, begging me for something I didn't know how to give. "What if I wrote him a letter?" I asked. "To let him know it's okay to just let go. I believe we all control the time and manner of our passing, but we don't know that we can just let go and it's over—just make a decision to go to sleep and not wake up. Maybe he just needs permission—a little nudge. What do you think?"

From the moment I'd started talking Mary had been vigorously nodding. "Yes! Write it. Right away. Please! I'll take it to him."

I went home and sat down and scribbled some notes. Then I wrote the letter that follows, as tears ran down my nose and dripped on the paper.

Dear Tom,

From what Mary tells me, you're lying around in bed loafing. We miss you out here on the trail. It would be great to have you back hiking with us again. If you feel you can return—and really want to—we'd love to have you back. Keep on fighting.

But if you're just too darn tired and it's not worth the struggle, it's okay to just kick back and let go. You're not a kid anymore, though your sly jokes and good humor have always made you seem like one. No wonder they call you "Otter." You're so sleek and slim. To me, you've never seemed anything but young. That's why I've always called you "youngster."

You've had a good life, Tom. You've got nothing left to prove. If there isn't very much to look forward to anymore, and it's getting too tuff to hang on, why not take a rest? It's okay to say "enough!" Just give yourself permission to let go and enjoy the big relief at the end of the trail. You've earned it. Just go to sleep deciding to wake up in heaven. You can do it. We all can. That's how I plan to go.

After all, it isn't the end. There's a great new existence waiting up ahead. I've heard it's truly wonderful on the other side—more like heaven than hell. If we don't see you again, thanks for the memories of all those good times we've shared over the years. We'll look forward, dear friend, to seeing you again—on this side or the other—here or hereafter.

So be good to yourself and do what deep down feels best.

Happy trails, Your buddy, Bob

The next day Mary called to report "When Tom read the letter he smiled and I could see him relax. He held onto it while we talked and when I spoke to his nurse I saw him read it again. When I came back that night he told me he'd read it over and over. He wanted to know what I thought, and we talked about it. I told him I agreed and it was okay with me...I think it's working."

She asked if I had any suggestions for helping him. "Talk to him awhile about dying each time you visit," I advised her. "Keep gently giving him permission to pass. Assure him you'll be perfectly okay when he's gone. Tell him it's time to be selfish, to put himself first, to do what *feels* right. Help him believe his life has been successful and complete, with nothing left to prove. Keep assuring him we all have a basic human right to leave when we want. He only has to make the decision to let go. Tell him death is a friend that will instantly wipe out all his fear, guilt, doubt, blame, frustration and inhibition—bringing unimaginable relief. Each time you leave, say a casual goodbye, so he knows he's free to leave before you return. Tell him you hate to see him unhappy and in pain. Remind him all he has to do is shut his eyes and go to sleep—it doesn't have to be night—expecting to wake up on the other side. And he will."

Two days later she called to tell me Tom had died the night before in his sleep. I found I felt happy for him. She credited the letter for helping him let go. I felt good about that because it meant I'd finally been able to help him, after all.

Months later, it dawned on me that a refinement of this simple approach to dying could prevent untold—and unnecessary—human suffering for many others. In fact, anyone who was seeking a better, easier way to go—and was open to new (actually old) ideas and attitudes—could make use of it. I had access to compelling source material that I thought would convince even a skeptic. I felt anyone could learn to release the life force that keeps us all alive. This powerful belief system wasn't radical or secret, but it wasn't well known either. I'd heard that enlightened individuals had used it for centuries, and spiritually aware people who knew how to create and live their lives deliberately were increasingly rediscovering and using it today.

It had long ago transformed my own attitude toward death from typical fearful denial to actual anticipation of an adventurous new beginning. I'd decided I wouldn't wait until I was helpless. I'd put the quality of my continuing life on the scales against the exciting fresh start waiting for me on the other side. When the scales tipped decisively toward exiting this lifetime, I knew I could simply release my life force at will.

As this knowledge took shape within me, it brought great and unexpected relief, giving me a new fear-free appetite for life. I felt I'd found a way to escape one of mankind's greatest miseries, and I felt I could briefly explain it to others, to give them the same option.

It wasn't long thereafter that I hatched the idea for this book.

~

"*All our knowledge merely helps us to die
a more painful death than animals.*"

–MAETERLINCK

"The fear of death is more to be feared than death itself."

–PUBLILIUS SYRUS

3

DEATH,
AMERICAN STYLE

Death is merely the end of life. It can be natural or voluntary. The individual must choose. "To be or not to be," as Shakespeare's Hamlet put it, "that is the question." Natural death is simply waiting to die. Voluntary Death is either suicide or Assisted Suicide. Suicide can be either: (1) An individual intentionally ending his or her life by killing the body—an undignified exit that's currently legal if unassisted but frowned on by society and condemned by many churches, or (2) Letting Go of Life, the peaceful, gentle dignified release of the life force described in this book. It's not only legal, it's completely undetectable and thus free of all stigma.

Assisted Suicide for the physically suffering can be divided into: (1) Physician Assisted Death, in which a doctor writes a lethal prescription but the patient administers it—legal at the moment only in Oregon, but apparently not for long. (2) Voluntary Euthanasia, a lethal injection by a doctor—legal only in Switzerland and The Netherlands, (3) Pulling the plug, i.e., "removal from life-sustaining medical treatment"—currently legal for the incurably dying when properly arranged.

The Right to Die Movement currently favors Physician Assisted Suicide for mentally competent, terminally ill adults who voluntarily request it. They claim the choice of death over life is an inalienable right of all mankind, our ultimate civil right. Patient's rights advocates maintain that people are entitled to the autonomy of decision-making and the personal integrity to be free of bodily and governmental intrusion despite the powers of those who philosophically disagree. The movement's goal is to make assisted death a legal viable alternative to an incurable helpless life.

"RIGHT TO DIE" HISTORY

Over the past two decades, America has been the battleground for a major political, social, cultural, and religious war over the fundamental question of our rights regarding death. Rising public awareness of suffering patients who lack all hope of regaining a meaningful quality of life manifests increasingly in demand for a dignified death in preference to intolerable life. That demand grew out of spiritual awakening, cultural and economic changes and shifting priorities, as well as unmet needs—reflecting the decline of the doctor-patient relationship, the economics of health care, and the medical profession's lax attitude toward pain control and comfort care.

The right of the terminally and incurably ill to choose an assisted death in recent years has overtaken abortion as America's most contentious social issue. Americans have come to fear a prolonged death at the hands of a cold, impersonal, arrogant medical technology that diminishes their dignity and emotionally and financially burdens their loved ones when no reasonable expectation of recovery exists. Though three-quarters of the public supports the right to physician-assisted death, that right is increasingly and ever-more-vigorously opposed by the establishment—our government, the Roman Catholic and fundamental churches, the American Medical Association and other institutions whose control it threatens. The result is that the suffering individual's right to die in the time and manner of his choosing is steadily shrinking.

The Right to Die Movement got its formal start back in 1980 with the formation of the Hemlock Society by Derek Humphry. Now boasting a membership of more than 25,000, it is dedicated to education and change as it relates to self-deliverance. In 1991 the movement got a shot in the arm (sorry) with the publication by Humphry of *Final Exit* which explicitly and chillingly set forth the pros and cons of dozens of inventive ways to kill yourself. The book brought suicide out of the closet in America, enjoying 18 weeks on the New York Times best-seller list, though it remains banned in some foreign countries, notably France.

The sudden appearance on the right-to-die scene of Dr. Jack Kevorkian in 1990 transformed the previously polite debate over the ethics of dying into an in-your-face fight when the retired Michigan pathologist offered death-on-request with a homemade "suicide machine." He polarized the country by publicly delivering the corpse to the medical examiner's office, then describing to the press exactly how death had occurred. In eight years he put a merciful end to over 130 willing sufferers before being sent to prison in 1999, where he is serving 10-25 years for second degree murder.

Though he outraged many, his general public approval rating remained high, suggesting the public's fear and condemnation of the sorry state of death in America at the end of the 20th Century. Despite the shocking nature of his actions, he's warmly regarded as a modern American hero by many for braving the church and the law to perform voluntary euthanasia to help suffering, terminally-ill patients die in what reasonable people seem to consider justifiable, compassionate circumstances.

OREGON STEPS FORWARD

The Oregon experience reveals a lot about Death American Style. Riding the right-to-die wave of public sympathy, the citizens of Oregon in 1994 voted (51-49%) to enact a Death with Dignity Act that would permit physicians to prescribe a lethal dose of a controlled substance (usually a barbiturate) under well-defined and restricted circumstances for certain terminally ill patients. The Act gave patients the right to self-administer the drug—with no further help from their doctors. Threatened opponents in the church immediately pounced. They succeeded in blocking implementation of the Act, but after years in the courts the identical measure went back on the ballot in 1997. This time it passed 60-40% and became the first and only law permitting physician-assisted suicide.

In between the two votes, the U.S. Supreme Court unanimously found that while there was no constitutional right to physician-assisted suicide, there was nothing to prohibit it either. So the question was explicitly referred to the "laboratory of the states," leaving them free to legalize it. But the zealous Federal Drug Enforcement Administration immediately stepped in to intimidate Oregon doctors by threatening to take away their licenses if they prescribed lethal drugs, alleging violations of the Controlled Substances Act. In June 1998, Attorney General Janet Reno came to the rescue by ruling that physician-assisted suicide under Oregon law would not violate federal drug laws.

An Oregon governmental agency report on the first year's experience with the law showed it to be effective and efficient, with no sign of abuse. None of the dire predictions of its opponents materialized. No hordes from other states flocked in to die. The poor and elderly weren't driven to suicide in droves. The drugs worked as expected and no suicides were botched. Only fifteen Oregonians used the law to end their lives, but others doubtless drew solace from knowing they could obtain ultimate relief if the pain got too great. The second year's experience was similarly uneventful. As a by-product of its strong focus on improving the end of life, Oregon now boasts the best palliative care in the country.

Despite the law's obvious success, another insidious effort has been launched to thwart it, this time in Congress. An amendment to the federal Controlled Substances Act, ironically called the Pain Relief Promotion Act, passed the House on October 27, 1999. Better known as the Hyde/ Nickles bill for its sponsors, Representative Henry Hyde (R-IL) and Senator Don Nickles (R-OK), both Roman Catholics, the bill would make it a federal crime, punishable by 20 years in prison, for doctors to prescribe drugs for patients to end their lives. Aimed squarely at killing the Oregon law, the Act expressly overrides Janet Reno's decision to defer to the voters of Oregon and other states. The bill is expected to pass the Senate and be signed into law by President Clinton before this book is printed.

Far from relieving pain, the measure would cruelly increase it by intimidating doctors everywhere from prescribing or administering doses of drugs adequate to relieve the pain symptoms of the millions of terminally ill patients who have no interest in physician-assisted suicide, as well as those who have! Under the bill, doctors would be forced to think twice about adequately prescribing barbiturates by the possibility of long prison sentences if their intentions are misread by government snoops. Thus, treatment of pain for the terminally ill, already notoriously inadequate because of society's exaggerated fears of drug abuse and addiction, would grow intolerably worse as doctor and drug scrutiny grows.

In summary, the bill holds that it's okay to hasten death, but only if that's not the physician's intent! Compassionate doctors trying to fully relieve their patients suffering, could be put in jail for 20 years for murder for their mercy! The AMA, of course, supports the bill. Not surprisingly, opposition to it has made strange bedfellows—doctors who see it as absurd and meddlesome, proponents of states' rights, Right-to-Die advocates, The Massachusetts Medical Society, which states that it would have "a chilling effect on prescribing adequate medicine," and the Oregon Medical Association.

Even Oregonians who voted against the Death in Dignity Act resent this attempt by Congress to casually dismiss it. The Supreme Court may be called upon to make the final determination. In the meantime, Congressmen Hyde and Nickles, in the service of their church instead of the people, must carry the responsibility for all those suffering in pain for lack of barbiturates. They suffer because the church fears the precedent in Oregon might somehow someday threaten its iron control of its parishioners. So if you can't get the drugs you need the next time you're in pain, you now know who to thank!

STATE OF THE UNION

As the century turns, our prevailing attitudes toward

death are positively Neanderthal, still solidly rooted in ignorance and fear. Institutions in the business of controlling people—the church and state—reinforce our primitive beliefs about death, resulting in untold suffering for the American public. Some religious teachings equate death with sin, while the state suspects that any death may be illegal. Old-school science, with its rationalist, materialistic, reality-based attitude has contributed to narrow rigid attitudes toward death. (The blessings of the new physics haven't yet trickled down to the public.) And parents innocently do their part in passing along the "bad news" to their children.

The result is that death in America is viewed as irrevocably, irredeemably BAD. Death is guilt and shame; it's the heavy penalty for living, the final failure and the ultimate punishment. Our culture strictly instructs us to wait helplessly and do nothing until death finally comes. The resulting monumental pain, cost and indignity don't signify in the least. If you try to help yourself or others die, you're sinning or breaking the law. We're sentenced by society to endure any misery, accept any horror, without lifting a finger to end the suffering—indefinitely. In this "land of the free and the home of the brave" our rights regarding death are far from free. Our Right To Die lags far behind our right to live. And when it comes to "brave," we're so petrified of death that we steadfastly deny it.

Nothing is so black and white in America as death. If you're young, your death is a terrible inexplicable tragedy.

And it's just as unforgivable if you're not certifiably terminally ill. The good, the famous and the beautiful people are not allowed to die either. The society-approved prescription for permissible death is simple: it's okay to die if you're in mortal agony, or terminally diseased, or extremely old and debilitated. Looking ghastly helps. Any other circumstance may arouse public suspicion, risking condemnation, shame and guilt, sin and illegality—for all your friends and relatives as well as yourself! Your death must conform to society's warped and baseless beliefs.

Because death is uniformly bad in our culture's view, it's okay for the bad to die—in fact they should. After all, we kill people who kill people, and jail people who help others end their lives. Death is the ultimate punishment. There are all kinds of restrictive laws about death. People are not supposed to kill themselves or help others end their lives. That's both sinful and illegal because it offends society.

Indoctrination in death's badness begins in childhood. Parents buy into the conspiracy of secrecy and denial offered by society, innocently joining the church and state. In time, however, the secret begins to seep out and kids must be given sugar-coated explanations, euphemisms, half-truths and outright lies. When death can no longer be denied, it's soft-pedaled. But the shocking truth of Death American Style finally hits—usually sometime during adolescence. One day we realize that someday we're going to die—and the horror stories and monstrous myths that abound scare us half to death. (I vividly recall when the gruesome realization struck me. I was 16. My depression lasted for weeks.)

When we make the great discovery of our mortality, we somehow change. Something wonderful dies within us. The unlimited innocent hope and optimism of youth, the belief that we can have or do or be anything, our sense of personal immortality—are all gone forever. (Teachers "from the other side" say this shock releases a "death hormone" that begins the aging process.) The rest of our narrowed and limited lives are spent unconsciously—or consciously—waiting for death, preparing to die.

We live our lives in the shadow of death. Life runs downhill toward death. Our death expectations begin the aging process that we're taught is sadly inevitable—but honorable. We spend the rest of our lives letting our body slowly decline, unconsciously preparing for our ultimate but respectable death. For perhaps 60 years we live with the brakes on. Finally, we obediently create the bodily deterioration and terminal illness or other approved (and probably painful) condition that allows us to satisfy society's criteria for acceptable death. If we can't stand to play that game and are willing to defy society, the only alternatives (until this book) are suicide and euthanasia.

Suicide threatens all segments of society because it highlights the culture's failures, so society retaliates by condemning suicide. But suicide rates are climbing steadily among older adults—an indictment of both society and the tyranny of death in America. Officially, there are some 30,000 suicides annually, but experts say the real figure is 3-4 times that high. Some dare to hint at the truth—that every death is a suicide.

No one wants to look closely at suicide. It's a threat to us all. We're more comfortable with murder because it's easier to explain. The result is a sanitized cover-up and an adamant denial of death. A bigger indictment of society comes from youth aged 15-24. One source says their suicide rate has risen 284% in 30 years. Clearly kids don't think much of the conditions they live in. Suicide is a rebellion, a protest, a demand for something better—from both youth and adults. Despite the contrary conditioning of a lifetime, they instinctively know they have a right to something better.

In Australia in 1998, young men were killing themselves at a greater rate than ever before, according to the Australian Bureau of Statistics. Men aged 25-44 had the highest suicide rate in the country, even higher than men 85 and older. Suicide among this group ranked second only to traffic deaths for youth as the country's leading cause of death.

Robert E. Neale in *The Art of Dying* explains that suicide breaks an implicit contract between the individual and society. Society claims this betrayal threatens the general stability. Suicide is a critical judgement on the culture, revealing its possible failings and limitations, denying its sacred values. It dares to suggest that there might be room for improvement. Society can't tolerate the suggestion that it might be sick, so it brands the suicide as sick. Theology sees suicide as an attack on God, a sin under the Commandment, "Thou shall not kill." The church much prefers that your death come from accident, war, disease or natural disaster because such circumstances don't imply criticism, don't reflect unfavorably on the status quo. Because suicide might represent the hope for a new and better community, it threatens both church and state. Neither look kindly on independence, much less a possible call for change. Anything that might promote freedom or spontaneity threatens institutions of every kind.

Euthanasia, a more genteel and less violent brand of suicide, has also risen in popularity. Dr. Kevorkian has brought it out of the closet and into the limelight. Its big drawback is that the church, the state and the medical profession have made it illegal, thus stealing your right to die when and how you choose. You need a doctor partner (who's breaking the law), or a lot of lies and deceit to squirrel away a big enough hoard of the ever more tightly controlled super sleeping pills required. (The establishment isn't about to make death easy just to ease your suffering. It might threaten their control.) Even with enough poison on hand, it's advised that you put a tight plastic bag over your head to make sure your breathing stops, because there's nothing worse than bungling your suicide!

JUST LET GO OF LIFE

This book offers a vastly different and infinitely more dignified option.

Primitive suicide and euthanasia are both aimed at brutally killing the poor innocent body (like killing the messenger), rather than merely releasing the life force from within it—the way enlightened people do. In this crude, undignified and ugly procedure, both suicide and euthanasia deny the eternal nature of the self (soul, spirit) despite the impressive evidence supporting both immortality of the soul and reincarnation. Modern science now adds its powerful endorsement to the concept that life is eternal.

Wait til you hear what the veterans of many deaths in Chapter 5 think of Death American Style. They sympathize with our understandable ignorance about death, because we haven't experienced it lately. But they shake their heads in wonder at our overpowering fear and hate of death. To them it would be laughable if it weren't for the tragic and useless suffering that results.

How did we reach this sad state of affairs?

Earliest man learned to worry because of his ability to think. The ability to make associations, to link cause and effect, to connect events in his mind and reach conclusions, also made him vulnerable to fear. Blessed and cursed by a higher consciousness than his fellow animals, he came to understand the nature of threat. Not yet at the top of the food chain, he spent most of his life trying merely to protect himself and survive in a desperately dangerous world. Nevertheless he was intrigued by death and quickly developed strong beliefs about it.

Over fifty thousand years ago, Neanderthals took to burying food, tools and ornamented shells with their dead. Corpses in some graves were buried in a fetal position and stained with red ochre. The ancient Egyptians viewed death not as the end, but as a transition from this world to another. Every early culture seems to have built ceremonies and rituals around death. During the Middle Ages, Christian churches rang their bells to notify the community that someone had died—and to prevent evil spirits from invading the body. From the very beginning, death was the mystery supreme, a source of awe and fear, and a fertile field for myth. Because of its mystery and great importance, beliefs about death proliferated. No culture was without its strong beliefs about death.

ORIGINS OF POWER

Because man's brain could link cause and effect, and because life was dangerous, it didn't take long for elementary psychology to manifest in response to the urge for self-preservation. In even the smallest and most primitive societies there were clever individuals who sought power over others. They soon saw the mystery and fear of death as a source of extra protection from life's plentiful threats. By developing power over their slower-witted fellows, they could get them to do more of the dirty work. They realized that power derives from the ability to control others. And even those primitive brains figured out that control comes most readily from manipulating weaker people through their fears. Offer them protection—or the illusion of protection—from what they fear most and they'll willingly obey, thus reinforcing the safety and authority of the protector.

The next step to building society was for leaders to set forth rules, laws and scripture, then requiring compliance as the price of benevolent protection. Leaders simply translated their own fears into laws that would protect them. Even today, laws are only as strong as the penalties for their disobedience, so punishments were assigned for crimes to ensure compliance. Police came into being to obtain that compliance. As government evolved, death was always in the mix, a powerful source of fear—and therefore a source of power. It became the ultimate threat for failure to comply. "Do as you are told or be killed."

As societies grew more sophisticated, the crude threats of torture and death were supplemented by the more subtle threats of hellfire, damnation and suffering in the afterlife. Sins and taboos were defined in great detail. Hell and purgatory were invented to keep the populace in line. Because the hereafter was even more mysterious and unknowable than death, a hideous afterlife could safely be invented and threatened with impunity, since no one could prove it didn't exist. Clever psychology increasingly joined or replaced brute force in designing belief systems and religions that would dependably control their followers. Nearly all religions came to use fear-based, death-oriented, afterlife punishment and reward, to preserve control and loyalty and gather needed wealth and support. In the earliest societies, work and play were often combined. Business and the church had not yet grabbed control. Play was an integral part of work and regimentation was unknown. Then came the reformation and the industrial revolution of the 16th Century in Europe. The deeply repressive new Protestantism and the Calvinist and Lutheran doctrine of self denial as moral purity effectively destroyed individualism, replacing it with the Protestant Work Ethic. Commerce and the church conspired to take control of everyday life. Shame and guilt became weapons for ensuring conformity, magnifying the role of fear in controlling the masses.

By the 19th Century, Western civilization was thoroughly poisoned by the new social consciousness. Individual freedom shrank when the church condemned pleasure and insisted that "original sin" condemns all children to remain as unhappy, ignorant and enslaved as their parents. American Puritanism, being opposed to the joy of living, squeezes those who fail to conform and yields the mottos of the 90s, "Pay your dues," "Earn your way," and "No pain, no gain."

With this shift in world morality, the repressive values of the church gained power, filtering down into government, the schools and finally to the heart and core of society—the family. Institutional authority grew rapidly, squeezing the joy and freedom out of life. Life hasn't been the same since the Reformation killed fun and spawned shame and guilt to bulwark fear and repression. Fear of embarrassment has grown so great that one recent poll showed that many individuals felt that death was often preferable to public embarrassment!

Thus, our culture has succeeded in controlling our views of death. The public today is still afraid to challenge the establishment's absurd, unproven disastrous view of death. Sadly, we've become a nation afraid, ruled more by our fears than any other ethic. We worry about what *might* happen and do what we *should* do, dragged down by continuous vague anxieties. We've given away our power, accepted shame and guilt, and knuckled under to society's disapproval.

In this sad state, our relationships fail, we watch our neighbors to find out what's socially acceptable (politically correct). We can't seem to relax, society's greatest blandishments somehow fail to satisfy, and happiness seems to elude us. We're frustrated, irritated, loveless, joyless and vaguely discontented. And we can't pinpoint why. To compensate, we grow more permissive, hedonistic, sexually active and attracted to drugs. But nothing seems to satisfy. Our frustration and neurosis often lead to alcoholism, rage and violence.

On the outside, society appears wonderfully free, but on the inside it's uptight, anxious and confused. Western culture has failed to mature, and our society is stunted. We enjoy a level of personal liberty unknown elsewhere in the word, but it brings us little contentment. Caught between pleasure and guilt, we don't know how to live. The constant conflict leaves us frozen, unable to choose between instinctive desires and the restrictions of society. Technology has left us freer than ever before, but we're pathetically unable to translate our new toys and capabilities into much pleasure. We're both freer and more repressed than the world's other cultures.

All this is reflected in our sad attitudes toward death. We hate them but we're helpless (until now) for lack of an optimistic alternative. So we settle for denial by making death taboo, because we fear it. We childishly pretend and sanitize, using euphemisms like "passed away," "gone over," "departed." Anything death-associated, like aging and terminal disease, are called by other names. We cosmetically color and cover-up, spending millions on surgery, diets and dyes. Death, like sex, is a secret to be whispered.

Everyone is afraid to let the dying know what's happening. Death must be sugar-coated and depersonalized. We're scared to death of death, because we think it's the absolute end of all opportunity, and we therefore equate it with failure and disaster. We deny death in hopes it will somehow disappear and go away. Even medical professionals can't talk straight about death. But the surrounding mystery and fear keep death endlessly fascinating. TV dramas feature it liberally at its most romantic while the horror films make it gruesome, and the news makes it ugly and sad. Good guys die easy, bad guys die deservedly hard. The depiction of death is always dependably warped.

Our persistent fear and fascination have produced a

vast literature of death. It's as gloomy and grim as it is biased and ignorant—somber instruction on how to grieve and mourn, wild, utterly baseless conjecture on what happens during death represented as cold hard fact. It perpetuates public ignorance and fear, but what's infinitely more damaging is the insidious repetition of hidden assumptions that all this blarney is inescapable, unavoidable bitter truth. That's what drags us down and inclines us to accept society's terrible prescriptions as fact.

No one here on earth has experienced death in this lifetime, so most of what we read about death has no basis in experience. It's a response to the insatiable hunger for crumbs of knowledge about the unknown—or the urging of some establishment authority with its own well-concealed, self-serving agenda. All we really know is that it's the end of physical life, the expiration of the body. That's about it. The rest is fear, hope, fear, superstition, fear, myth and more fear.

Author Neale, for instance, tells us that there are nine distinctly different fears of death: (1) the fear of body decay, (2) fear of judgment by God, (3) fear of the unknown, (4) fear of pain, (5) fear of indignity, (6) fear of being a burden to others, (7) fear of loss of control, (8) fear of incompleteness and unworthiness, and (9) fear of separation. Implicit in this list is the (western/Christian) assumption that fear is an essential inextricable ingredient in death.

Dr. Elisabeth Kubler-Ross subdivides death—after the obligatory terminal illness—into five stages: (1) Denial,

(2) Anger, (3) Bargaining, (4) Depression, and (5) Acceptance. This depressing but well-accepted scenario seems to summarize society's view of the sad state of death in America today.

Another author offers us four degrees of suicide: (1) any direct means, like taking poison or jumping off the roof, (2) long delayed self-sabotage: i.e., nasty habits of self abuse like alcohol or drugs, (3) recklessness: e.g., playing chicken, (4) war, crime, accidents and natural disaster. (Note how eager these authors are to organize and quantify death to escape its unnerving mystery and subjectivity.) To this gloomy list I would add a cheerful fifth: (5) the peaceful and deliberate release of the life force from the body, as taught in this book.

When it comes to denial, nothing can surpass our hilarious treatment of the corpse in a vain and ludicrous attempt to pretend death was dignified. We pay undertakers to do a makeover on the often ravished body so that it looks so healthy and respectable that relatives who were present in the last days don't recognize him or her. Then there are lavish caskets to match the cosmetic restoration.

Death must be made tasteful at all costs—and the costs of all this folly are considerable. The most ludicrous aspect of this undertaking is that everyone pretends in an unspoken conspiracy that what Jessica Mitford called, "this sad, rouged hunk of embalmed decaying meat, the dear departed," is still the (now long-gone) person we so recently knew and loved. Finally, we're obliged to pity and mourn the tragic passing, which was probably long overdue and doubtless brought blessed relief.

A few short decades ago, the vast majority of Americans died peacefully at home in their beds. The family doctor, not yet threatened by malpractice suits and the high cost of insurance to protect against it, gave what help was needed and looked the other way, or gave Gramps a little unseen nudge if necessary.

That was before the vast arsenal of drugs and high-tech apparatus for saving lives was perfected. Though designed "to extend youth" (e.g., save the resilient young from the results of their disastrous automobile accidents), this technology came to be forced on the old and ill and helpless who have no hope of recovery and would rather not survive as comatose vegetables while their life savings dwindle, drifting toward a ghastly and undignified end.

Doctors routinely placed patients on life-sustaining systems when there was no real hope of producing more than a subhuman existence. Life sustaining treatment to replace or support a failing body function is defined as any medical procedure that prolongs the dying process by artificially supplying respiration, nutrition, hydration, etc.

Gradually, the medical community developed a "technological imperative," which obligated doctors to use whatever medical treatment was available, regardless of the potential benefit to the patient or the high emotional, mental, physical or financial cost. Patients routinely received unwanted and unwarranted high tech intrusive treatment, but were denied comfort-providing medications and human contact.

Doctors continued to play God with their technological systems until 1976 when the judge in the *Karen Ann Quinlan* case ruled, for the first time, that Americans had the right to make prior arrangements to "pull the plug." Karen had been in a persistent vegetative state for years, yet her doctors, despite court orders, refused to withdraw her respirator and let her die. The court's decision to free her from useless life revolutionized the medical profession and led to laws in all 50 states allowing living wills, health care proxies, or both, the first step in right-to-die public policy.

But enforcing these instruments can still be difficult. While studies show that many physicians approve assisted suicide and voluntary euthanasia, many more hide behind the AMA, which remains militantly opposed and has a long and shameful resistance to change of any kind. Other studies show that many doctors neglect, even avoid, patients they feel they cannot cure. Effective pain medication exists, but the will and skill to use it are sadly lacking, thanks in large part to the intimidating vigor of the Federal Drug Administration and its allies in Congress. The relief of patient suffering also remains low priority in our medical profession due to a lack of training in medical schools.

Nowadays, unfortunately, over 80% of deaths occur in hospitals or nursing homes, where the individual is virtually powerless to control anything that happens. Gramps just lies there while the meter runs, eating up an average 40% of his lifetime expenditure for health care. If you're not blessed with feisty relatives armed with all the needed Living Wills and Durable Powers of Attorney to dictate what you will and won't tolerate, you're absolutely at the mercy of the institution's expensive whims. Nevertheless, desire is so desperately great to escape this costly, painful, total loss of control, that some 70% of deaths are "arranged," for the terminally ill who no longer can speak for themselves, i.e., patients are mercifully taken off life-support systems and allowed to die.

NEAR DEATH EXPERIENCES

The closest we come on this planet to actual knowledge of dying comes from Near-Death Experiences (NDEs). Accounts of these brief glimpses of the beyond are not only remarkably consistent with one another, they fit comfortably with what the experts from the other side (whom you'll meet in chapter 4) tell us happens when we die. There is often proof of the veracity of these accounts in the form of special knowledge that couldn't otherwise be explained. NDE testimony agrees that what dependably comes first after death is unbelievable freedom and sweet relief. Every care disappears with the shedding of the body. Then there's a welcome return to wisdom, joy and long-lost friends, followed by a delightful sense of expansion and the insightful confirmation that each of us does indeed create his own reality.

The usual scenario in an NDE (as viewed from the outside) is that someone living dangerously or having a heart attack actually dies, is pronounced dead, then is somehow resuscitated by doctors. From the inside, the victim seems to be dreaming in an intensely real manner and is generally floating above the body, calmly and objectively (even amused) observing. He typically reports hearing loud noises, moving effortlessly down a tunnel, being greeted by bright but not blinding light and a familiar religious figure who seems to know every embarrassing detail of his life yet exudes forgiving love. Though NDE individuals enjoy only the briefest taste of the afterlife, they are often transformed by this experience, finding new joy and purpose in life, and reveling in freedom from any fear of death. (Much more on NDEs will be found later.)

That quick snapshot of what awaits us is consistent with the picture painted of the first stage of death by those who've actually died and speak to us through channels. Note the contrast between this peaceful portrait and the horrors portrayed by the purveyors of Death American Style—featuring the church's frightening depiction of hell and purgatory!

But happily there are signs of hope that dying conditions in America are improving. Dr. Kevorkian and Derek Humphry are leading the rebellion against the sad state of death in America today, steadily gaining sympathy and votes for a genuine Right to Die. Quantum physics is breaking the stranglehold of many outmoded concepts and beliefs. The new physics, once it trickles down through the schools to the public, could eventually undermine many of our primitive beliefs regarding death as well as life. It has already put a firm scientific foundation under para-psychology by putting the physics back into metaphysics. And people timidly are opening to new possibilities. What with Dr. Kevorkian, death legislation and the publicity for hospices, death is being discussed as never before. Dying is coming out of the closet.

But there isn't any need to wait around for society to finally adopt a truly emancipated, enlightened view of death. Overcoming all that fear—not to mention the resistance of the church and state—promises to be a glacially slow process, so it may not happen in your lifetime or that of your children. Fortunately, there's no need to wait for another millennium. A solution is now at hand.

~

*"There is something beyond the grave;
death does not end all."*

–PROPERTIUS, 54 BC

"Our souls survive this death."

–OVID, 43 BC

4

INTRODUCING CHANNELS
The Only Real Authority on Death

What do we really know about death? Not much. We know it's the end of our physical life, the end of our body. That's about all. The rest is hope, fear, superstition, hearsay, myth and wild conjecture. Self-appointed authorities tell us what we ought to believe about death, but they haven't been there. They don't know any more than we do. No one here on earth really knows what death is like.

But there is one dependable authority on the subject. Many of the people who have died and now speak to us from the other side through channels are happy to explain death and dying from actual experience. They've been there—more than once—so they speak with an authority that can't be matched.

Don't groan. It may be fashionable to bash channels, but that's because we've been taught to be distrustful of what we can't see. "Seeing is believing" and "Once burned, twice shy" are the mottoes of our fear-based society. We've learned to be wary, cautious and afraid of the strange and unfamiliar, threatened by anything radically different. And channels are definitely different. People claiming to speak for the dead are bound to evoke skepticism, especially if their eyes are closed and their voices sound a little strange. Clever movie makers in Hollywood, by capitalizing on our fear of what's strange and unfamiliar, have taught us to distrust channels. And comics love to pan them.

Fearing the unfamiliar is understandable but not essential. There is no growth without change, no security without daring to face what you fear. The way to get past the strangeness of the source is to simply remind yourself that strange voices can't harm you, so it really can't hurt to listen. After all, because the source is brand new to you, and the subject matter interests you, you might learn something valuable! So forget about the strangeness and suspend your disbelief long enough to listen to the message and see what *you* think. Better still, pay attention to how the message makes you feel. Trust your judgement instead of letting preconditioned fears block you. Don't deny yourself out of habit and irrational fear. Forget the strange source and trust yourself to make independent judgements. It could change your life—and your death. It certainly did for me.

Thoughtful people down the ages have found channels to be a truly valuable source of reliable information on many subjects. Channeling is as old as civilization, but it's often been known by other names. Christianity since its beginning has smiled on paranormal occurrences like angels, voices, miracles and divine revelations. Great artists of every kind have relied on inspiration and tapped into the unknown reaches of the mind to access the creative genius. Philosophers and psychologists have relied on intuitive insights. Even scientists credit channels for leading them to discoveries.

I've learned a lot from them in the 15 years I've been listening. In the beginning I was distrustful, even disdainful of what a bunch of "spooks" could possibly teach me, but I was open enough to put my prejudices on hold and temporarily suspend judgement. The message made sense to me right from the start. I was fascinated by what I heard—it was new and exciting—so I gradually forgot the strangeness of the source. Instead of turning off, I decided to test the message. When you receive advice that sounds good and feels good, tests out and makes you prosperous and happy—as it has for me—you soon come to respect the source.

What the channels in this book have to say about death and dying will excite you, because of the wonderful hope they hold out. They make "the other side," where they dwell, sound positively enchanting—with no sign of anything resembling hell. They say the closest thing to hell that they've encountered is on our side of the fence!

When I speak of "channels," I'm not talking about palm readers, crystal ball gazers, phone psychics, fortune tellers or carnival entertainers. I'm talking about those worldly wise, respectable and dependable communicators from the non-physical world who are regularly consulted by statesmen, bankers and captains of industry. So, if you want insider information on dying and death, how to control your peaceful passing, and what to expect on the other side—suspend your doubts and listen to the only authentic authorities on the subject.

But first let's take a close look at channeling and respectable channels in hopes of dispelling some of the strangeness and mystery that so easily evoke the disdain, suspicion and distrust we've been taught. My principal source/authority is William Kautz, former staff scientist for Stanford Research Institute, founder of the Center for Applied Intuition, and co-author with Melanie Branon of *Channeling, The Intuitive Connection.* The dictionary tells us a channel is a course or passage, a route or means of access. In the case of humans, both physical and discarnate (i.e., non-physical), it's a way for those on the other side to speak to us on this side. It's merely how the dead talk to the living.

Kautz says, "Channeling is an age-old intuitive practice—with a universal, but unseen source of information and insight." So it's also a way to access the otherwise hidden wisdom within each of us. Well-known channel Kevin Ryerson, who wrote this book's introduction, says "Channeling is a not-so-mysterious way of tapping into the intuition with which you were born." It's a mental process in which the channel partially or totally sets aside waking consciousness in order to allow discarnate entities (i.e., non-physical voices from beyond) to take over. Non-physicals are called entities because their voice may represent one person or many.

Kautz explains that competent channels come from every walk of life, are of any age and every degree of education. They are ordinary people who have discovered or developed a latent ability to pick up the thoughts projected by non-physicals. Some become aware of their powers in childhood. Others laboriously train until they become adept at receiving. What they have in common is a devotion to refining their intuitive skills to the necessary level of expertise, plus the ability and inclination to receive, and a motivation to help humanity. It means they have skillfully learned to set aside subconscious blocks and fears in order to open up a clear channel to the superconscious and beyond. They have learned to calm the conscious mind, relax the body deeply and completely, and let their tension flow out and away. Masterful meditation then takes their calm mind to a state of "nonthinking" where the ego gives way to an awareness of the universal reservoir of knowledge and intuition.

This intuitive information arrives in any of three ways, through major sense preferences: by sight, sound or touch. But generally it comes in clear impulses of thought which the channel then interprets and translates into words. Because these thought impulses are filtered through an individual human being, three different channels would deliver very differently phrased messages from the same set of thought impulses. The words you hear reflects the channel's education, vocabulary, personality, clarity and character as well as his or her ability to interpret and translate those thought impulses into words.

There are two basic types of channels. "Light trance" channels (also called "sensitives") simply tap into a higher state of consciousness or impersonal reservoir of knowledge, says Kautz. No personality change is obvious in them. They talk almost normally, speaking from a slightly meditative state. Esther Hicks is a light trance channel, shifting from her own personality to that of Abraham with seeming ease after a dozen years of experience. Her eyes are open and her voice change has become minimal.

(My wife and I had a memorable four-hour dinner with Esther and her husband Jerry, during which Abraham, seemingly observing and eager to participate, easily and frankly came in and out of the conversation! It was strange but delightfully stimulating, and fun!)

"Deep trance" channels, on the other hand, close their eyes and appear to fall asleep as they enter an altered state of consciousness, allowing another personality or spiritual entity to emerge. Kautz explains that these entities frequently possess distinct vocal qualities, mannerisms and personal characteristics that may be quite different from the personalities of their channels. Jach Pursel, who channels the well-known entity Lazaris, whose work I studied for many years, is a deep trance channel. Letting Lazaris come through takes longer and seems more difficult for Jach than letting Abraham speak through Esther.

Channeling takes place during two typical situations: group generalized lectures and individual, one-on-one counseling called "life reading." Most channels usually do both. For example, my favorite, Esther Hicks, who channels Abraham, travels around the country with her husband Jerry, giving weekend group workshops, but the subject matter discussed is determined by questions from the participants. And before she got too busy, Esther used to be available for telephone consultations to individuals by appointment. (Abraham is a group of teachers dedicated to helping us. They speak through Esther with a single consensus-view voice.)

Good channeled entities do not claim to be final authorities. They are merely guides to show you options for choosing your path wisely. Your mind can be a receiver to many forms of thought. Channels are here to help us broaden our own perceptions, to help us know ourselves better by whatever means work best for the individual.

ACCEPTING & UNDERSTANDING CHANNELS

There are four main belief criteria that make accepting

and understanding channeled entities easy: (1) When your body dies, your soul (spirit, character, personality—all that you've learned) moves out and lives on in the non-physical realm. Your body is not the real you; it's just a physical shell. It grows old and wears out as you steadily grow wiser, so the two of you are going in opposite directions. The body, as someone said, is "just the cage of self-protection in which we fitfully live."

Nowadays, believing in some kind of afterlife is common. Many Western religions accept the concept of immortality, and eternal life has been well documented in respectable parapsychology journals. Modern scientists, applying quantum physics, now know that there can be no endings, so clearly life goes on after death.

(2) An afterlife is the foundation of the concept of Reincarnation, the idea that we get born again to experience another lifetime. And we keep repeating the cycle. We live many lifetimes here on earth, inhabiting a succession of bodies over the ages. Three-quarters of the world's population believes in reincarnation, and recent studies show conclusively that a majority of Americans have come to accept the concept, too. The new physics now lets scientists accept it as well.

(3) It therefore follows that in between physical lifetimes our true eternal selves are alive and well in the nonphysical realm, out of sight but not out of touch. Though they currently have no bodies, they can talk to us through the channels they've chosen to serve as vehicles for their thoughts.

(4) We've all died many times but each time we return for a new life, we leave behind the memory of all our prior lives—parking it out of our reach on the other side. That's something we willingly agree to before returning to physical status through birth for another lifetime. Once we die and pass back into non-physical, that vast memory of infinite lifetimes returns. That's why channels are so wise. They have access to the wisdom of the ages, accumulated over a great many lifetimes. By contrast, our best thinkers can only access their experience from this lifetime.

If you can accept these four beliefs, or can muster an open mind—or merely manage temporarily to suspend your disbelief—you'll find the channeling of entities from beyond quite easy to accept. If you find it hard to believe that what you're hearing comes from people who have died and re-connected with the wisdom of their vast memory, just focus on the *content*, not the source. Suspend your judgment but notice your feelings about what you hear. See how good the message makes you feel. That's the real test. If what you hear feels good, it has to be right for you. Don't narrowly limit yourself to "Seeing is believing." Wise men know it's the other way around: you must first believe—or suspend disbelief—in order to truly see.

Now hear what four highly respected channels—featuring my favorite, Abraham—have to say about death and dying from the authoritative perspective of those who've been there many times. The Abraham group's purpose and pleasure is to help us struggling physical beings cope, grow, and pursue freedom and joy. Other channels tap the same or other groups of teachers or individuals on the other side. Their consensus view on How the World Works is as reassuring as it is remarkable.

These teachers are eager to explain how the Laws of the Universe affect us, and how new understanding can help us take back control of our lives—and our deaths. Theirs is an utterly different belief system from the fear-based hodgepodge we've inherited. Let's call theirs *The Universal View* ("U-View" for short). It's consistent and comprehensive but wonderfully simple, and it applies to all circumstances and situations without exception. Our Earth View, by comparison, is inconsistent, haphazard, action-oriented and undefined, with more holes than Swiss cheese, riddled with gaps and puzzling contradictions. Its myriad exceptions and loopholes reflect our blind, naive belief in fate, chance, luck, accident and coincidence. Ours is a collection of unconnected and often contradictory beliefs rather than a comprehensive system that can answer all questions. It doesn't really qualify as a Belief System, but it's all we've had—until now.

When we discover how things really work, we see why we fail to achieve what we most want in this world—including control of our deaths. Because the U-View is so simple and all-inclusive, we soon see how we can use it to deliberately take control of our lives to achieve the success and find the happiness and freedom we seek. With control of our lives, it follows that we enjoy the same control over death—just as we did with our birth.

The belief system we're about to explore is the foundation, the framework, for taking control of both life and death. It's something concrete to build on. It won't take long to explain it. You'll soon see how to sensibly use the U-View to clean up your act and stop shooting yourself in the foot. You'll see how to stop doing things that sabotage your happiness and success, replacing them with simple strategies to avoid major setbacks. Instead of just "letting things happen," you have the power to deliberately create what you want, reclaiming your life and setting the stage for controlling your death.

From my personal standpoint, to give you human perspective, I encountered this system of belief about 15 years ago while listening to the channeled entity Lazaris. I had tried out a lot of religions, philosophies and belief systems over the years, but none of them came close to fitting. I was marking time as a pantheist when I encountered the U-View.

To my amazement, it fit like the proverbial glove, right from the start. I had always assumed that ready-made belief systems were like cheap suits off the rack, they never quite fit. You had to forge your own beliefs, one at a time— the work of a lifetime. However, once I put the U-View into practice, major setbacks stopped afflicting my life, permitting success of every sort to manifest, bringing me a level of freedom and happiness and prosperity I had never known before.

So please park your skepticism and anxieties about accepting guidance from people you can't see. Listen with an open mind to astounding good news from the experts on easy transitions. You'll find their perspective is more specific, authoritative, exciting and optimistic than anything you've ever heard about death and dying from our earthbound spiritual leaders. I guarantee—if you're open—that you'll like what you hear, even if you find it hard to identify with the messenger.

In the following chapter you'll find an overview of what the experts on the other side reveal about How the Universe Works—and our part in it. That will lay the groundwork for expansion in the chapters that follow of the key points that form the framework for taking full control of your death. You may even find—as I did—that it's worth testing this prescription for happiness and success to take back control of the rest of your life!

Now get ready for the good stuff. The fun's about to begin!

$\sim$

"*A good death does honor to a whole life.*"

–PETRARCH

"Death shall have no dominion."

–DYLAN THOMAS

5

THE WAY THINGS WORK

N ow comes the good stuff, the Universal View of all creation, as reported through the channeled voices of the wise beings residing in non-physical. We'll call them "the experts." Once physical humans like us, they now have access to the wisdom of the ages—and their generous loving intention is to help us.

As the chapter title suggests, wise beings in non-physical don't see The U-View as merely the best belief system going. To them it's the *only* view, cosmic truth that rules both physical and non-physical worlds impartially and completely. From their insider's view, it's How Things Really Are, ground zero, the root of all knowledge. They see a comprehensive system that's not to be compared with the jumble of fragmented, competing inconsistent belief systems, religions and world views that we have clumsily created here on earth. Belief, after all, is merely conditioned, repeated, codified experience. What they offer is far beyond that.

Sound too good to be true? I don't blame you if you're skeptical. You've been burned before, so it's natural to be suspicious of yet another panacea. We've been offered so many, and they've so often disappointed. Everything we try turns out to have major flaws and fails to work, much less satisfy. After having our hopes repeatedly dashed, we're reluctant to risk yet another letdown.

But this one is different, and there's a way to test it without risk. You test it (and anything else) by simply listening with your heart and your feelings, not just your brain. If it feels right and excites you or makes you feel good, you can safely proceed. If it doesn't, reject it, and you've lost nothing. Trust your feelings. They'll infallibly guide you.

It will readily be seen that The U-View bears little resemblance to our haphazard belief systems. Because it's unfamiliar, it's first being presented in the form of a condensed profile, a digest or summary of the main points in logical sequence, starting with the Universe and working inward toward its effect on the individual and his or her life and death. I've arbitrarily divided the indivisible—with apologies to the enlightened—to promote clarity and understanding. Clarity and comprehension are the goals of this compartmentalized overview.

In the chapters that follow, parts of the puzzle will be elaborated and expanded to construct the framework and foundation for taking full control of your peaceful natural exit from this life. So park your skepticism and listen with your feelings as well as your brain to this 13-point overview. You're in for a treat. Here we go!

1. THE UNIVERSE IS GOOD

When we say "universe," we mean God, Goddess, All That Is, or whatever term you like for the infinite power and source of all creative energy. At first glance, this assurance of dependable, loving goodness may not seem profound, but when you let it sink in, it can yield a lot of comfort. Many have sadly come to believe (fear) just the opposite: that the Universe is somehow malevolent, something evil to beware and guard against. When we look around us—or at our problems—it's easy to fear that we're in constant jeopardy and must struggle to protect ourselves against evil. We sometimes wonder whose side the Universe is on. Are "they" out to get us? When you're down and feeling like the world's turned against you, it's reassuring to remember that All is Well, the Universe loves us and Well Being Abounds.

The Universe continually flows its positive creative energy toward us with the intent of making us happy, healthy and successful. If we relax and stop shutting out that powerful flow with our fear, negativity and resistance, we'll be showered with nothing but good, without any effort on our part. The Universe wants the best for us in every respect. It's pointing us, pulling us, toward health, happiness and success. All we have to do is park our fears, listen to our hearts and get out of the way. All TRULY is well.

2. WE ARE EXTENSIONS OF THE UNIVERSE

Which means we're an integral, inseparable part of the goodness. The Universe is within each one of us. We are interconnected with it and therefore connected to everything and everybody else. No one is separate or alone or outside it. Understanding this connection reinforces the goodness and potential for success. Because the Universe is a force for good, and it's within us, we're beneficiaries of that goodness, too.

Your link to the non-physical realm, where the workings of the universe are clear, we'll call your Inner Being or Higher Self. It lives within you as a wise and loving agent of the non-physical Universe. It's always trying to help you, guide you, point you down the path toward fulfillment. This is your spirit or soul, the ageless, eternal you that has been your companion through all your many lifetimes. Though you have no memory of those lifetimes at present, you have indirect access to their accumulated wisdom through your Inner Being. It speaks to you through your emotions. This infinitely wise inner you is always talking to you through your feelings. It's always nudging you toward success and health, toward choices that fulfill the broad intentions you held when coming into this lifetime.

Since we're each an extension of the Universe, it lives within each of us. In fact the experts urge us to become more selfish, not more humble and selfless. To realize our purpose we need to take greater charge of our lives, make more choices, express more desires, be guided by our feelings, not by other people or institutions.

3. YOU'RE IN THIS LIFETIME BY CHOICE

It's not by accident or whim, or as a punishment for past failures, that you're here in this lifetime. After hanging out on the non-physical side for awhile after your last lifetime and death, you got restless (we're told) for another opportunity to experience the great contrast offered by life on earth. It offers an unparalleled stimulation and opportunity for excitement and adventure, a chance to explore and grow. So you deliberately chose—with eager anticipation—to return for another lifetime to co-create with other humans. You chose to come back because you wanted to, not because you had to.

You didn't just land here by accident, either. You carefully chose the situation into which you would be born. It had to fit your intentions. You carefully chose your time and place of birth, your parents, your sex and nationality. None of this was fate or chance, karma or luck, accident or some dutiful obligation. You deliberately chose it all. Whatever your current problems or regrets, be assured that you came here willingly—and the problems can all be solved.

4. YOU CAME HERE WITH AN AGENDA

You came back to earth with great intentions and well-defined purpose—not on a lark or out of boredom. You came with the broad intent to experience time and space and the joys of physicality, to fine-tune the process of deliberate creation through thought, to add to your knowledge and that of the Universe. It's a glorious time on this planet for creating, says the channeled entity Abraham. There is so much contrast, so much to choose from, so many important decisions to be made. You came eagerly and deliberately, to be joyful and uplifted, to be a part of the leading edge, in search of unique, emphatic and personal experiences. You wanted more of the contrast and sensuality that is found here.

You also came to grow through certain more specific pursuits. When you're feeling good, that's your Inner Being telling you that you're on track with those pursuits, allowing yourself more of what you intended. To feel good and stay in the groove, you need only to appreciate the world and the people around you—and to avoid negativity.

5. YOUR PURPOSE HERE IS TO FIND FREEDOM AND JOY

Mankind struggles mightily to find some serious purpose in life—usually by proving worthiness to others—a terrible mistake according to the experts. The U-View explains that our broad and specific purpose in coming back for another lifetime always involves seeking freedom, having fun and experiencing joy. Feeling Good, plus mental and emotional creating, not action, are what produce success of every kind—as well as happiness, freedom and joy. Action alone does not create.

It may sound too simple to be true, but feeling good is both the end and the means.

Attitude and belief are everything. Without accompanying appropriate belief and expectation, action (like work) is virtually useless! Work only works (i.e., seems to create) when your work intentions and expectations and enjoyment of what you do are in harmony. If you hate your work or don't believe it will create real success, be assured that it won't. All you'll ever get is a paycheck.

6. YOU CREATE WITH THOUGHT AND EMOTION

Now that the cosmic foundation has been laid, we zoom in to the nuts and bolts human perspective—to be expanded in Chapter 6. Here we address the problems of the individual. Now you learn to create what you want.

The big news is that we create our reality—every event in our life—with our thought and emotion, not with action (like work). That's a radical shift in belief for most of us and may take some digesting, but it's a concept that's heartily endorsed by modern science. The ramifications are immense and profound. One of the biggest immediate benefits of this U-View of creation is the safety it offers. If we alone create everything that happens to us, we have to be totally safe from others—and they from us. So there's nothing left to fear! Others can't harm us. Harm from any source can't touch us without our permission. And that permission can only come from our fear!

We're totally in charge...not only free of reasons to fear

but free from the worrying uncertainties of fate, luck, chance, accident and coincidence. They don't exist—unless you create the events they represent. You have the power to control what's created. And because we can't create in the lives of other individuals—only they can do that—we're free from the vast responsibility of trying to fix things for other people. We're also free from the shame and guilt that come from failing to take that responsibility. Since we can't create for others, we're free of the need to seek their approval—or anybody else's.

7. YOU CAN BE OR DO OR HAVE ANYTHING

If you create everything that happens with thought, and if there are no limits to where you can direct that thought, then it follows that you can create anything you can imagine. Anything! No limits! Just make the choices that sharpen and focus your desires. Apply the formula above—deliberately and without the resistance of worry and doubt—and anything you desire can be created. No kidding!

Asking yourself "why" you want a particular desire to manifest will help you sharpen your desire and add the catalyst of feeling. Passionate desire creates more quickly and surely. Strong feeling attached to your desire prods the Universe to make it manifest. The more intense and pure (i.e., without doubt) your feelings, the faster and more surely you'll get what you desire. Abraham is fond of saying, "It's as easy to create a castle as a button." Allowing others to create as *they* wish will also help allow the manifestation of *your* desire.

8. FOLLOW YOUR GUIDANCE SYSTEM

Each of us has a wise, loving Inner Being at the core of our true, ageless, eternal self. It's patiently watching, eager to guide us. It persistently but subtly nudges us along the path that leads to our goals (i.e., the broad and specific intentions we held when coming into this lifetime). It also serves as a guidance system that renders an opinion on the merits of any course of action we're engaged in or considering. To get a verdict (or at least a hint) we have only to consult our feelings on the subject.

Its message won't be printed on a billboard. Bells won't ring. But if you're sensitive to your emotions you'll get an indication. If you're ecstatic, you know you're in complete harmony with your intentions. (That's how I feel about writing this book!) If you feel the slightest twinge of any negative emotion—apprehension, repugnance, anger, doubt, sadness, disappointment, wariness, etc.—anything less than excitement, joy or enthusiasm—you're being warned against the contemplated course of action. You'll know by how you feel if you're on course.

If you repeatedly ignore or fail to accept its guidance, your Inner Being will pull the plug on its free advice by disconnecting you from the stream of positive energy from the Universe. You'll feel unlucky or plagued with problems. Being wholly positive, the Universe cannot relate to negativity. The flow of positive energy that creates what you want is cut off at the source when you engage in negative thought or action—like anger and fear. When you're disconnected, you've not only lost the positive flow, you've lost the guidance of your Inner Being—a double-barreled loss!

When you ditch the negativity and jump back on the positive bandwagon, your Inner Being eagerly returns to help you. You can feel it. And it feels good. So develop an awareness of your feelings by intending sensitivity. Then make the choices that feel good. And give Feeling Good top priority in your life. My motto: "*Nothing* is more important than feeling good!" When you Feel Good you're totally connected, and the universe is working hard to make you feel even better. And Feeling Good brings success in all that you desire. That's all you need to know to create. If you forget everything else, remember to Feel Good and you can't go wrong.

9. DELIBERATE CREATION OF WHAT YOU WANT

Earlier, we learned the procedure for creation—thoughts and emotion, not action, create. It's the Law of Attraction, the Number One principle of U-View. It says you are constantly creating your life with the balance of your thoughts and feelings, whether you want to or not, whether you know it or not. The process never stops. You get what you attract. What you attract is dictated by the balance of your thoughts and feelings. Your life today is a reflection of all the thoughts and feelings you have held throughout your life, a living portrait of what you've attracted over a lifetime. Look in the mirror. Do you like what you see? If not, here's a chance to make some changes.

You can continue to take pot luck, i.e., create randomly according to whatever pops into your head and heart, driven by your current beliefs (and sabotaged by worry and fear)! Or you can harness the Law of Attraction to deliberately create what you want, taking back control of your life. If your life has been less than you hoped and you want to make some changes, you must change the pattern of your thoughts and feelings. That in turn may require changing some of the habits and beliefs that cause you to attract things you really don't want.

When you begin to control your thoughts and feelings, deliberately choosing those that match what you want, you are Creating Deliberately, sitting in the catbird seat, in full control of your life. The Universe *must* respond to your every intent and expectation. It's a law. Expectation and intent focus both your feelings and thoughts. The focus of your attention also attracts. So pay attention to where you put your attention. Ask yourself whether your thoughts and feelings are focused on things you really want to attract. If you don't like the answer you get—if you're focused on what you fear—maybe that's why you don't like the way your life is going!

Garbage in means garbage out. And a lot of what we give our attention to is garbage. To test the desirability of giving something your attention, ask yourself, "Would I want to attract that into my life?" Try it out on the evening news. We're picky about what we eat and how we dress, but we dangerously give our attention to what we hate and fear! We need to be much more discriminating about what we give our attention to! The bad stuff can do a lot of damage.

10. BELIEFS ARE EVERYTHING

There are no facts, only beliefs. What drives and dictates your thoughts, feelings, habits, attention and expectations are your beliefs: a lifetime collection of often unconscious and forgotten experiences that affected you so strongly that they imprinted themselves on your consciousness as fact. They came often enough or with sufficient force to convince you that they were true. Ever since they became beliefs they've been unconsciously dictating your actions and reactions. You are the sum of your beliefs. They are your master. You must obey. Science heartily agrees, declaring that there is no truth, only observers and observations.

Unfortunately, a great many of these beliefs, perhaps the majority, have a negative effect on your life, severely limiting your attraction of success. Many of your beliefs, because they're unconscious, are in direct opposition to what you say and do—and think you believe! You think one way but the your beliefs point you in another direction. That's how strong and dangerous they are. They're quite capable of undermining your life without your realizing it. These limiting beliefs are the chief obstacle in your path. They cause you to attract all the things you don't want.

Your best initial defense is to deliberately hold the intention that they come out of the shadows and reveal themselves to you. You can't get rid of them until they're identified. Abraham urges us to ask the Universe to reveal any beliefs that are limiting the manifestation of your desires. (You'll learn other ways to identify, isolate and demolish unwanted beliefs in chapter 6.)

11. EVERY DEATH IS A SUICIDE

Now that we have a framework of creation sitting solidly on the foundation of How the Universe Works, we're ready to consider how all this applies to death and dying. Because you create your every moment with thought and emotion, according to your choices, you can deliberately choose to die at any time. Just relax and allow your passage back into the non-physical realm. Your soul, spirit, lifetime memories, personality and Inner Being will make the trip with you. They constitute the eternal life force within you. They are life everlasting. Your physical body is just the shell you inhabit during this lifetime. It is not you. It stays behind. Only your body dies. The real essential you lives on, intact.

Don't mourn for Grandma's death. She picked her spot, made her choice and let go. Instead of grieving, which is negative and harms you (and doesn't help her) celebrate the wonderful euphoric relief she enjoyed at the moment of her passing, when every care and woe of this lifetime was magically lifted. That's what I did when my mom died in a faraway hospital. There's no greater relief on earth, says Abraham.

"Every death is a suicide," they say, defining suicide broadly as do-it-yourself death. Though at first that statement sounds harsh and shocking, the reasoning is simple. If nothing happens by accident, all events are determined by the Law of Attraction. If everything that happens is a result of your choices, it therefore follows that you choose your death. It's Law! Every death represents a decision. In fact you *can't* die until you've made that decision! Even deaths in so-called natural disasters (floods, famines, volcanos), all accidental deaths (drownings, car crashes)—even murders—are the result of making the choice to die or being willing to let go of life. The actual circumstances of your death aren't attracted until after you've made your choice.

Not only do you always make the choice to die, you can't die, it turns out, *until* you've made that choice! That's confirmed by the consensus experience of people who have survived Near Death Experiences (NDEs), people who should have died (according to medical experts) but didn't. NDE's are individuals who reached death's door and got a glimpse of the afterlife, then returned to life instead of dying, because they weren't yet ready to leave. They came back to life, says Abraham, simply because they hadn't yet made the decision to die! They were just living dangerously, or in the wrong place at the wrong time. They believed they were safe, and so they were. They believed they wouldn't die, and so they didn't. That shows the power of beliefs. "Beliefs," insists Abraham, "are quite literally everything."

12. YOU CAN DIE WHEN YOU WANT

Now that we've established that you only die by choice, it follows that you can make your transition when you want. It's okay to leave while you're still healthy—considered blasphemy in this culture! It's even okay to leave when you're young! There's no law that says you have to be sick to die. In the face of this heresy it may ease your mind to know that Abraham explains, "It was never your intention to be here very long. Living isn't a contest to see how long you can last. That's just a belief that's entrenched in your society."

Our purposes here can best be accomplished, they say, when you're vigorous and young, not when you're old and worn out. Cultural pressure is so great in our society, says Abraham, that it actually causes us to attract pain and illness in order to justify leaving, so we can die miserable and helpless but respectably! That's how intimidated we are by society's ability to make us feel shame and guilt! We're so afraid of what others may think if we let go of life while we're young or healthy that we hang on as long as we can.

Abraham says, "You think you can't leave in good grace until something really bad happens to you. You have to get sick or old or decrepit—or run over by a car." A long life, they tell us, wasn't our intent when we decided to come back for this current lifetime. It was usually our plan to make the transition back to non-physical while we're still healthy and happy, but ready for a change, feeling our work here is done. But usually we don't do that. We tend to hang around as long as possible because we're so afraid of others' disapproval. This dependency on the good opinion of others is one of the biggest obstacles to creating what we want in this lifetime.

13. HOW TO PASS PEACEFULLY WHEN YOU CHOOSE

Most people postpone the decision to let go of life until they simply can't stand living any longer—until they have no other choice. But a choice must be made, and nobody else can make it for you—despite appearances to the contrary and common cultural beliefs. The decision to let go is often unconscious, but you can make it conscious. And you can go a step farther by deciding on the circumstances of your passing. You can decide to draw your last breath in your sleep or while conscious—alone or with your mate— or after a party with friends. But these are subordinate choices. Wise channeled voices from beyond supply the ways and means of "letting go" in greater detail in Chapter 8.

The experts agree that your ease of transition will depend on your attitude at the end. People die, we are told, the way they live. If they approach death kicking and screaming, fighting and disbelieving, fearful and resisting, their transition will initially be difficult. If they surrender peacefully, with acceptance and anticipation of the grand adventure that lies ahead, their passing will be infinitely joyful and delicious. They will savor the ecstasy of instant relief with a joy beyond all description.

There you have it—The U-View of THE WAY THINGS WORK in a nutshell. In Chapter 6 we'll take a longer look at how we create with thought and feeling, expectancy and attention—and how to use this knowledge to live deliberately for greater freedom, joy and success. Taking control of your life in this fashion lights the way for controlling your peaceful natural death.

~

"There is no death! The stars go down
to rise upon some other shore."

–JOHN MCCREERY

"There is no death! What seems so is transition."

–HENRY LONGFELLOW

6

CREATION
IN A NUTSHELL

Before jumping into the exciting world of creation, let's take a quick look back at the foundation and framework we have built. It begins with our insistence on our absolute right as individuals to full control over every circumstance of our passing, a sort of ultimate Declaration of Independence. If you've given that control away to others, what follows may make you reconsider!

I've tried to show that wise, respectable, channeled voices from the beyond are the principal, authentic, reliable authority we have on the subject of death. Not only do they have memories of innumerable deaths, they have the wisdom of the ages at their disposal—and a generous loving willingness to help us comprehend. Contrast that with the insistent urging of our human leaders—who often have their own agendas and who have no actual memory/experience of death themselves. Take your pick.

But you don't have to take the word of the non-physical experts. It may surprise you to know that contemporary science—more specifically the new quantum physics—heartily endorses a great many of the assertions of our best channeled entities! Our culture has come to rely on the logical, concrete explanations of science. It's become our principal source of dependable, comforting beliefs about "what really is" and "how things work." What science says is accepted as fact and truth. It's the supreme authority on which we depend. So it's comforting to learn that the new views of modern science corroborate the U-View.

The authority for these new beliefs is quantum physics, the foundation of modern science, which had its formal beginnings in the 1920s, building on the discoveries of Albert Einstein. Quantum physics explained the formerly inexplicable transformation of nonmatter into matter, time into space, and mass into energy. In the process, it revealed that we humans have our origins in thought, not matter. Thought, we're assured, produces both the body and mind. Science insists—as do the experts on the other side—that it's thought, not action, that drives all human creation.

Human beings originate, it's been discovered, as a field of non-material intelligence or inner awareness. It's this intelligence, propelled by thought, that produces what we know of as reality. The mind, it's now known, resides in every cell of our bodies, not just in our brains. And all our cells regularly communicate with one another to create the unfolding events of our lives. That's the new scientific basis for creation: our thoughts, not our actions, determine our conscious reality, our awareness. Each of us builds our lives, brick by brick, with our thoughts, not our actions. The mind is always dominant over the body.

The quantum view becomes easier to understand when you forget the old barriers between body and brain and drop that outmoded distinction. A division between the two no longer exists (and never did). Just think of every cell as "bodymind." The bodymind concept permits the new scientific world view—and U-View—that we create solely with thought. We are thoughts that created bodies, not physical machines that somehow learned to think. Every thought you hold manifests physically in the body. That's why negative thought produces afflictions and disease. Constant worry creates illness. And it's a constant process, one that can't be stopped. So it pays to pay attention to the focus of your thoughts!

The balance of your attention, says science, determines what you get. Because thought alone creates, you alone are in control. That means you can be or do or have anything you want—if you deliberately hold unmixed thoughts and expectations. Quantum physics has discovered that we don't really accomplish much through action, work and struggle—unless our thoughts are in harmony with our goals—because it's the thought that's doing the creating! Focused attention, pure desire and genuine expectation are what create the events of our lives, our successes and our failures.

But that's not all. Quantum physics also validates the insistence from beyond that there can be no death—except that of the earthly body. If death were complete it would be the end of consciousness, but it's been proven conclusively that consciousness doesn't end because time does not flow. Science has discovered that the passage of time is only an illusion, a belief we have embraced for the sake of convenience. Einstein wrote, "...the distinction between past, present and future is only an illusion, even if a stubborn one." Because time cannot be bounded, death can not be final. So the life force, soul, spirit, personality and memories of this lifetime—all that's truly us—is eternal and everlasting. This cannot die.

Science further confirms that there are no facts, only observations and resultant beliefs. Truth doesn't exist because all knowledge is subjective. Einstein discovered there are only observers and their subjective observations. Nothing is real until it is observed. No event occurs until it has been witnessed. Reality is not fixed. Everything is inextricably connected to everything else. The universe is in a constant state of change. Nothing can be isolated. And mind is everywhere projected.

Deepak Chopra, MD, in his impressive bestseller *Quantum Healing* elegantly elaborates. The body reacts at the touch of a thought, he tells us. The body has a mind of its own. The whole body has intelligence and the ability to think, but it takes its orders from the brain. Thoughts turn into molecules through some hidden transformation accomplished by the presence of an impulse of the nervous system. When a thought appears, the brain's cells all change in sync to express it in the body. And this information travels faster than the speed of light.

To think is to form brain patterns that become body patterns. Thought makes matter. And the body remembers, reacting according to programmed thought, faithfully expressing past belief and expectation. An allergic reaction, for instance, is the body obediently reacting to codified past instructions based on fearful associations conveyed by the brain to the body cells.

Nature strives to heal and repair the body, to combat degeneration and continue life, which gives credence to the contention from the experts on the other side that the Universe is Good (Chapter 5), always flowing healing energy toward us with the intention of making us happy, healthy and successful. "The material body is a river of atoms, the mind is a river of thoughts, and what holds them together is a river of intelligence," sums up Chopra.

Bell's Theorem, formulated in 1964 and now accepted as a ruling principle of modern physics, holds that the reality of the universe requires that all objects and events in the cosmos are inter-connected. Nothing is separate; everything is a part of the whole. Or as English astronomer Sir Arthur Eddington was fond of saying decades earlier, "When the electron vibrates, the universe shakes."

These are the principal surface conclusions, interpretations and applications of quantum physics about how the Universe works. Beyond this point modern science rapidly becomes unintelligible gibberish to anyone but physicists. Try to look below the surface and there's a sudden drop-off into depths well beyond our ability to conceive. That's why quantum physics, for the most part, remains a total mystery to the public almost a century after it began to emerge. Take away familiar time, and the distinction between mind and body, matter and energy, and most people are soon lost. But modern science has corroborated the equally strange message from the world of our non-physical experts, strengthening both and making the pair a force that cannot easily be ignored or denied forever.

In recent decades, the discoveries of quantum physics have repeatedly been confirmed by independent findings of medical researchers and psychologists. And further corroboration comes from a wide spectrum of other sources—from ancient Indian philosophy to modern metaphysics. The result of this interlocking network of evidence is a new paradigm, a new view of the universe and the origins of man. Building on this new paradigm, it can be seen that deliberate creation of what's wanted will most dependably result from concentrated, passionate attention over time.

So truly we are what we think, not what we do. Thoughts, not actions, shape the course of our lives. What we think about and talk about most is what we get. Our lives are a combination of what we desire, expect and believe. Our thoughts are like magnets, continuously attracting the focus of our attention. That's the new paradigm of creation, according to the experts on BOTH sides of life!

WHAT HAPPENS WHEN WE DIE?

Voices from the other side tells us that when we finally make the choice to shed our mortal body and exit this lifetime, our whole life force moves easily out of the body and into the non-physical realm. There we pick up the vast accumulated memories, wisdom and experience of all our past lives. Then we rejoin old friends, and settle into a delightful new enlightened existence—non-physical but wonderfully stimulating.

Sooner or later, however, the itch for the stimulation of the physical life beckons. We yearn for the freedom and joy and fresh chance to grow through exploration and adventurous experience. As extensions of the universe—God/Goddess, All That is—we're eager to return to make the choices and decisions that add to our knowledge and that of the universe.

The experts tell us it may take anywhere from a week to a thousand earth years before we're ready to come back. Then it's time for complex preparations. First, we formulate broad and specific goals and intents for the coming lifetime. To implement these, we look for the perfect situation to be born into. In the process we pick our parents (a big choice), our sex, nationality, time, location, particular circumstances—everything that fulfills our intent.

When all is ready, we again park our vast memory, experience and wisdom in non-physical in order to start a fresh lifetime. Then we enter the growing fetus that we chose, usually just before its birth, and come down our mother's birth canal into that new lifetime. We repeat this cycle over and over through the ages, hopefully growing wiser with each cycle—learning by experience in this world, and from wise non-physical teachers on the other side—but always parking that prodigious memory before re-entering this world.

UNDERSTANDING PURE CREATION

Now that we're here again—with broad intentions for this lifetime—let's look at how creation works so we can understand why we get what we get, how we can create what we want, and avoid what we don't want. The experts on the other side offer a startling universal view of creation. They tell us that we alone create our entire reality. It isn't fate, luck, chance, karma, accident or the actions of others. We're totally responsible for everything that happens to us. Each of us creates every moment of our lives, and we do it with our thoughts and emotions, not with action. All that arduous work and striving and straining and struggling that we've been taught is so essential—doesn't really create! YOU CREATE EVERYTHING WITH THOUGHT AND EMOTION, NOT ACTION. No exceptions. Modern science, as we have seen, concurs. It's been conclusively determined that the mind creates all that we know of as reality.

Unfortunately, these new ideas tend to contradict everything we've heard all our lives, so they may take some digesting. To clarify, we'll first break down these concepts of creation with definitions so we can examine how they work. Then we'll make our way from the bare bones of raw creation to exciting ways of harnessing it to take full control of our lives—and our deaths. That's Deliberate Creation.

Our formula states that Thought and Emotion Create, but emotion is really just a catalyst that makes the equation work. It's Thought, not action, that creates. Emotion just makes it happen faster. Passionate desire creates powerfully, but so does worry and fear. "Thought" breaks down into such disparate concepts as Desire, Expectation, Attention and Beliefs. These are apples, oranges and pears, not equivalents. In raw or random creation, Desire is often only a weak or accidental ingredient, while in Deliberate Creation it's vitally important to maximize the intensity of your Desire.

Expectation—what we expect to happen—is more important. Our expectations are determined by our lifetime collection of Beliefs. Expectation is nothing more than what we believe will occur in any set of circumstances, based on those accumulated beliefs. Our beliefs represent the conclusions that we have drawn from our lifetime of experience. Thus our beliefs become self-fulfilling. What we believe creates experience that usually fits our expectations. This circular cause and effect keeps reinforcing our habits, making us resistant to changing our lives.

If beliefs are negative, it's a vicious circle, but if they're positive, the reinforcement will be a blessing.

Attention is merely "awareness," the focus of our thought at any given moment. Attention is an essential component of Expectation, in fact, it's a prerequisite. Without attention there is no expectation. Expectation is the marriage of Attention and Belief.

It will be helpful to get clear on these uses of Belief, Desire, Emotion, Attention and Expectation in order to understand what follows.

The raw concept of pure creation is based on—and driven by—the prime principle of the universe. It's called the Law of Attraction. Unlike the vague principles governing beliefs on earth, the Law of Attraction operates without exception; there are no loopholes of fate, luck, chance, etc. It continuously delivers the full content of our lives—every event—on the basis of our feeling, expectation and attention. It works like a magnet to attract the balance or focus of our thought, our hopes and our fears. Whether we like it or not, whether we know it or not, we're continuously attracting the events of our lives. We can't shut off attraction. It's the proverbial irresistible force. The universe orchestrates our lives according to what we think about most.

There are several ways to express the Law of Attraction. Simply stated it says:

Thought—i.e., Desire, Expectation and Emotion—Attracts (or Creates). It may be helpful to make this mouthful more visual and objective-looking—especially for practical, pragmatic, left brain readers. So here it is in the form of an equation:

If "D" is Desire, "X" is expectation, "E" is emotion and "C" is Creation, the equation reads, $D + X + E = C$.

Expectation Attracts—if there's no offsetting counter-attraction. Your thoughts are always drawing you toward the subject you're thinking about most—good or bad. The Universe guarantees it. (Unfortunately, thanks to a lifetime of contrary beliefs, there's a mine-field of negative attraction to be dealt with—most of which we create ourselves. We're often busily attracting just the opposite of what we want! More about that shortly.)

Another way to think of the process of attraction involves Attention. The Law of Attraction says that you attract into your life those events to which you give your attention, because attention is the pathway (or the path back to) experience and thus to beliefs, feelings and expectations.

It can be said that this Law directs the course of your life, attracting events according to your beliefs. Beliefs, as we saw, are the conditioned codified record of your lifetime experience, your interpretation of all you've encountered. They reflect your every conclusion and they determine your expectations. Your expectations are mere expressions and projections of your lifetime collection of beliefs. They continually dictate your actions and reactions. There are no facts, only beliefs. Beliefs are absolutely everything. Science, as we saw, heartily concurs, declaring that truth really doesn't exist, because all knowledge is subjective.

Our beliefs are deceptively self-fulfilling and self-reinforcing. As the observer of your experience, you interpret it according to your beliefs, ensuring that those beliefs remain unchanged. We unconsciously protect and defend our beliefs—because we believe they are us. And in one context they are. Even more insidious, because they're often unconscious, your beliefs may be diametrically opposed to what you think you believe. You intend one thing but they deliver another. They can undermine your life without your realizing the source of your trouble. Contrary beliefs can cause you to attract just the opposite of what you want. It happens all the time—to all of us.

Suppose you commute every day to work in your car on a congested road, taking other carpoolers with you, and you worry a lot about some crazy, drunk/drugged driver coming across the centerline and hitting you head-on. You anxiously, angrily point out swerving drivers to your fellow passengers, you watch chase scenes in movies that show deadly collisions, you listen to your insurance agent's grim auto accident statistics and you carry high collision coverage. You imagine what a crash would be like, even visualize yourself being injured, maybe killed. And you worry about it.

Then one day it happens. Your persistent, emotional attention and imagination, your fear of a collision, your belief in the danger and frequency of such collisions, attracts one. (It happens thousands of times each day, and it isn't fate, luck or chance!) Though it's exactly the opposite of the safety you wanted, you attracted it as surely as if you'd asked for it. In a real sense, you have. Your emotion, attention and expectation invited it. You're hurt in the crash, just as you expected, but your carpool passengers, who didn't share your persistent fear, escape uninjured because they didn't attract it!

Until now I have merely been describing the basic process of creation, how things work. Hopefully you've begun to get a glimmer of the matchless opportunity that this formula for creation affords for taking charge of your life—and death—by harnessing the Law of Attraction for Deliberate—instead of random—Creation. What makes that possible is its utter consistency and dependability. You can count on it.

So now that you know how creation works, you have two choices: (1) continue to let random thoughts and fears, old habits and contrary beliefs sabotage your expectations—and be prepared for continued random results; or (2) accept the gift and try harnessing this magnificent new tool. Deliberately create what you want by taking charge of what you think and feel in order to deliver a clear, strong, pure expectation of success. The Law offers the exciting hope, the unparalleled opportunity, of taking back control of your life to find the freedom, joy and success you desire. It's your choice.

One of the biggest benefits of this concept of creation for us earthlings lies in our relationships with others. First, consider the safety it confers. Because we alone create everything that happens to us, it follows that we are totally safe from others. "They" can't harm us—unless we attract that harm through our attention and fear. Without our permission, bad things can't touch us. We're exactly as safe as we choose to be. The means of control is in our hands.

So you needn't fear being mugged—as long as you refuse to be afraid while out walking, and refuse to give attention to potential muggers. You have to *feel* safe. If you feel safe, you are safe. And security systems and extra locks on your doors aren't needed to protect against burglars. Just don't fear burglars or ever think about being burglarized, and you're safe. Again, your thoughts and feelings dictate. If you feel safe, you are safe.

We're also the beneficiaries of freedom from responsibility for others. Just as they can't harm us, we can't harm or help them. We can't create in the lives of others because only they can do that. They each create their own lives, so we're free from the need to try to fix their lives. And we're free of the shame and guilt that come from failing to do so. We're also free of the powerful, destructive need to seek approval from others.

If your bossy mom tells you you're hurting her feelings by not doing what she wants, gently tell her that's impossible, because only she can decide what to feel. Refuse to feel guilty. You can't help her feelings. Forget the habit of "duty" and follow your own feelings. Finally, we're free from the fear of being victims of fate, luck, chance, accident, karma and coincidence. They don't exist. They're only beliefs. Those loopholes have been closed by the concept of individually creating everything that happens to us. You're in charge.

Because we create with thought, and there's no limit to what we can think of, it follows that we can be or do or have anything we want. ANYthing. Without limits. So why not give this system a whirl? There's nothing to lose and a lot to gain, like taking the fear and disappointment from your life and replacing it with happiness and success—and gaining a new control of your life—not to mention control of your easy peaceful death!

DELIBERATE CREATION

To put the Law of Attraction to work in your life you have to change the pattern of your feelings and thoughts, your expectations and the focus of your attention. You begin with an intention, a shift in attitude, a decision to make a fresh choice. But first a warning: Expectation has to be honest. You can't fake it because the universe is tuned into feelings, not words. What you truly expect is what you're going to get. Your true expectations will reflect your deep-down beliefs, not your current hopes and desires. That may help you understand why you have what you have up to now.

We've got a toolbox full of techniques to help you side-step the obstacles, most of which you have constructed yourself. The first tool is your Inner Guide (call it Inner Being or Higher Self, if you like) and the nifty guidance system it administers. This extension of the Universe runs on emotion, not thought.

It would be impossible to monitor anyone's thoughts. There's too much chatter and chaos, boiling ideas, nagging fear and erupting memories to ever edit out the poisoning negativity. Happily, you have a nonstop, all-wise, foolproof Guidance System that gives you an emotional reading on any action you're considering or involved in. If it feels right, that's your Inner Guide giving you the go-ahead. If you have doubts, feel reluctance, indecision or any other negative emotion, you're being warned against proceeding. The action in question, says your Higher Self, is not in your best interests. It's advising you to put on the brakes and reconsider.

Your Inner Guide is your ageless, true eternal self. Infinitely wise and loving, it wants the very best for you. It's waiting patiently to guide you, but it won't participate in negative action. If you don't hear or heed its advice it takes a hike, cutting off the flow of the all-positive energy that creates the things you want. To avail yourself of this invaluable guidance system, you need to look and listen for it in order to be aware of the subtle signals it's sending you. Develop a sensitivity to how you feel. Then make the choices that deep down feel good. They'll be right for you.

The second tool is choosing to Feel Good. When you Feel Good you're totally connected to your Inner Being, to the positive stream of energy and to your Guidance System. That means the Universe is working hard to make you feel even better and to make your desires manifest. I can't over-emphasize that Feeling Good brings success of every kind. It's all you have to do to be successful. If you forget the rest, make Feeling Good your top priority. It's both the end and the means. It's all you need to create, to turn your dreams to reality. And what could be better than Feeling Good all the time?

The best source of Feeling Good is Appreciation and Gratitude. Make it your intent to appreciate everyone and everything around you. Be determined to appreciate and you'll Feel Good all the time. Appreciation is the easy form of love, and it works just as well. Call it Gratitude if that makes it easier. If you want to Feel Good in a hurry under any circumstances, stop what you're doing, look around you, and find a way to feel appreciation for everything and everybody around you. Appreciate like mad! Start small with things and people you already like—working up to the harder stuff. When you can even find something to appreciate in your enemies, you're an expert appreciator. When I catch myself criticizing or judging, I try to find something in the object of my complaint to appreciate. It turns my mood around and makes me Feel Good.

The key to appreciation is letting yourself *allow*—not just tolerate—the world around you. Let other people be themselves. You'll find it's easier to allow now that you know they can't hurt you. They can't create in your life, so it's safe to allow others to do their own thing. You no longer need to feel threatened by others, so tell yourself you're ready to let go of that fear. Allowing is generosity. Like appreciation, it feels good.

ATTENTION INVITES ATTRACTION

You can help your positive attraction mightily by shutting the door on all the unneeded negative attraction in your life. Negativity doesn't feel good. Just ask your guidance system. Appreciating, Feeling Good and listening for guidance from your Inner Being will help you turn your back on bad feelings. Remember: attention invites attraction, so keep your focus on what you want to attract, instead of on misery, disease, fear, violence and anything else you don't want entering your life.

Fortified with your new knowledge of attraction, you can see the latent danger in watching horror movies, giving attention to war and disease, flood, rape, murder and all the other daily disasters on TV. Let your Guidance System be the judge. My rule of thumb: if a show or movie isn't dependably uplifting, with humor, likeable characters and happy endings, forget it. And don't hang out with people who insist on talking about doom-and-gloom topics. If you can't change the subject to good news, excuse yourself and move on.

The Universe isn't dumb or hard of hearing. When asking for your heart's desire, wait to do it when you're feeling so upbeat, optimistic and confident that no hint of doubt can creep in. Any sort of resistance (like doubt, anger, fear, etc.) will undo your attempt to attract and create. Remember, the Universe tunes in to feelings, not words.

When it comes to words, it's counterproductive to use "no," "not" or "never" in reference to something you don't want. Unfortunately, if you talk about what you don't want, it comes across to the Universe as the focus of your attention and expectation—and therefore it attracts! Refer only to what's wanted. And don't overdo it. The more you repeat your wishes, the greater the chance of including offsetting resistance. Desire can be pure but usually isn't. By definition, it contains the *lack* of what's desired, and that acts as resistance to positive attraction; i.e., you wouldn't want it unless you lacked it! So don't nag.

I call the next tool "Talk It Up." Suppose you have a persistent problem that keeps demanding your attention, dragging you down with self-perpetuating negativity, making you feel bad. Suppose you have a critical mate. Make yourself a list of all his good points, the things you're grateful for, what you appreciate about him. Then go through the list mentally or verbally when you're feeling resentful toward him, expressing the maximum happy emotion as you appreciate. It will make you feel good, diminishing your resentment. Focus on those good points, the qualities and habits you appreciate and admire. Talk up your good feelings of appreciation when you get down, and keep your attention and feeling off his criticism of you. It will lift your spirits and reconnect you with your Inner Guide and the energy that creates. He'll appreciate it, too, and will probably make more effort to please you.

When you're talking it up or trying to positively attract, it can be helpful to find innumerable answers to the question, "Why do I want it?" Searching for answers and explaining them to the Universe (and to yourself) helps keep the good feelings rolling. Creations of some kinds may manifest in mere minutes, hours or days. But healing chronic health problems, which were created over a period of years, will often take considerably longer. So be patient and talk up the good feelings to counteract persisting resistance. Don't worry or stew. A watched creation never hatches. Don't let apparent lack of results discourage you. If you obey The Law, the Universe must deliver.

Be relentlessly optimistic, a spin doctor determined to look on the bright side. Remind yourself frequently that ALL IS WELL and WELL-BEING ABOUNDS because it is and it does. Optimism is looking at trouble and seeing it as minimal, temporary and easily overcome. Be a Pollyanna. Laugh at trouble. Laugh at your serious self. Practice positive denial. Turn your back on so-called realism if it isn't what you want. It doesn't have to be YOUR reality. Your aim is to build the habit of positive expectation to facilitate creation of what you want—and to ditch the old habit of giving attention to negativity and lack.

How do you decide which tactic to use: Positive Denial or Talk It Up? Use the latter on persistent, habitual, chronic, reactionary conditions, troubles or physical symptoms, the things that constantly plague you. They will be the toughest nuts to crack. Use Positive Denial when your problem is sudden and unexpected, like an unpleasant surprise. Instead of negatively reacting, getting defensive, caving in, going ballistic, feeling trapped, getting ready to fight, or giving up—grab your lifeline of stubborn optimism. Turn your back on trouble, steadfastly deny it, laugh at it—and yourself for overreacting. Don't call it bad luck, accident, karma or fate. Belittle the problem as temporary and inconsequential and expect it to vanish. Admit you somehow attracted it, and deliberately turn your attention to something happy and engaging.

The channeled entity Abraham provides some amazing statistics to show that thought creates a million times better than action. They say it only takes 17 seconds of uninterrupted focused expectation before the Universe starts to manifest what's expected and expressed. So you can safely get mad—without attracting more anger and negative consequence—providing you don't stay mad for more than 16 seconds. I find that "grace period on negativity" quite reassuring.

On the positive side, hold pure expectation with passion—without a hint of resistance—-for 34 seconds and you've harnessed creative energy equivalent to 20,000 hours of work—that's 40 hours a week for a year! And the benefits increase exponentially. Stretch that to a pure

68 seconds and you've got the equivalent of over two million hours or 100 years on the job. That's how decisively deliberate creation beats merely taking action! It's not always easy to be purely positive in this negative world, but clearly it's worth the effort. As a bonus, it always feels good.

Whatever you do, don't forget the shortcut to creation: Feeling Good. You can always fall back on it, because when you're feeling good you're connected to the flow and the universe is working to manifest your desires. Feeling Good is the ultimate prescription for creating. It may sound too simple, but it's really all you need for success of every kind.

Now that we've presented the major tools at your disposal for Deliberate Creation, it's time to look more closely at the mine-field of resistance, the obstacle course that stands in the way of creation—most of which you've been building brick by brick for a lifetime. First comes the Big Three of personal Resistance: (1) Fear, (2) Destructive Beliefs, and (3) Low Self Esteem.

THE BIG BAD THREE

(1) By far your biggest obstacle is fear. Many people live in a state of fear, and even though it's often invisible, it's a factor in most of their decisions. Fear runs their lives— and many of our institutions too, though we work hard at denying it and keeping it from our consciousness. With all its euphemistic names and hidden faces, it's more than half invisible, but it's the bottom line of all negative emotion. Some people might admit to being concerned, uneasy, worried—even anxious, apprehensive or dismayed. But

they don't want to think about panic or terror no matter how desperate they feel. (Strong men aren't allowed to be scared or afraid. But it's sadly true that "most men lead lives of quiet desperation.")

The way to deal with fear is (a) stop denying and admit it, and (b) look at its sources, which are often irrational and based on beliefs you innocently adopted as a child and never replaced. Because the Law of Attraction shows we're really safe, it demolishes the need for many basic fears. So clearly intend to be free of fear. Fear can be defined as "anticipated loss or failure, the expectation that you won't be able to cope with some coming specific situation." Dragging fear out of the closet and into the daylight and giving it and its origins a hard look will often lessen or release its grip. The antidote to fear is simply Self-Trust. You need to build the justified belief that you CAN cope with whatever comes. You do this by refusing to let fear stop you. Face your fear and act in spite of it.

(2) Destructive Beliefs. Lurking behind our lifetime collection of destructive negative habits are the hidden beliefs that drive them. But how do we unearth, much less change, them? The first step is to acknowledge them. Admit what scares you or bugs you. The second is to adopt the firm intention of seeing and feeling those fears and destructive beliefs, dragging them out of the shadows and into the bright light of day. We are ruled by our lifetime accumulation of beliefs. They are nothing more than our interpretation of that lifetime experience. Your Guidance

System is subtly revealing them all the time—you only need to tune in. Once they're revealed, they can be changed.

Here's a proven technique for permanently getting rid of negative beliefs that afflict and haunt you. (1) In a quiet, private place, go deep within yourself to find a particular limitation, old habit, angry feeling or unwanted belief that you want to get rid of. (2) Go into the feelings and exaggerate them to the max, expanding the emotion until you reach some kind of limit. (3) When you run out of feeling, there'll be a viewpoint shift. You'll feel detached, dispassionate. You'll realize you don't have to hang on to what's unwanted. Now you're in control of your reality, not controlled by your beliefs. (4) Reinforce this discovery by telling yourself, "I'm free of this. It's no longer mine." You've now withdrawn the creating energy, disassociated and detached yourself from the unwanted habit, fear, belief. You ARE free!

Many people don't realize that feelings—how you feel at any given moment—are a choice, a decision. Often the choice is automatic, unconscious, driven by old habit, old belief and expectation. But you can consciously take charge—and make the decision to feel differently, to Feel Good. Remind yourself that "Nothing is more important than Feeling Good," especially when you don't. Invoke deliberate appreciation. Decide to Feel Good, no matter what. Create a smile—and a laugh if you can manage it—and good feelings will follow if you let them. To prime the pump, look for ways, things and people to appreciate.

(3) Low self-esteem, need of approval, dependency on others, guilt, shame, duty—all these combine to destroy the optimistic expectation needed to create what's wanted. Psychiatrists and therapists say most of our waking hours are spent in the often convoluted, neurotic pursuit of self-esteem. Unfortunately, that pursuit is spent fruitlessly courting the good opinion of others, seeking their approval, staying dependent on their validation of our worthiness. But it's a hopeless task. You can never please everyone. That's why we fail. We look outside ourselves for worthiness, not within. Look inside for strength and trust yourself.

Abraham teaches that the only reliable source of self-esteem lies within each of us. You have to believe in yourself, trust yourself, depend on yourself—ultimately love yourself. Instead of feeling guilt and shame about being selfish, you have to become *more* self-absorbed, self-reliant, even more selfish. The source of self-esteem is inside you, not outside. It has nothing to do with the approval of others. The source of self-esteem is Internal Validation. You'll find a host of easy techniques in my short, inexpensive book, *Have More Fun!*, for building self-esteem, banishing pessimism, fighting fear, identifying beliefs, changing feelings, attacking worry, learning to laugh—and much more. The trio of obstacles just discussed lives within the individual.

Now we take a look at Mass Consciousness, a totally invisible set of negative beliefs that reside outside us in society. These beliefs are so deeply embedded in our culture that they're often invisible and rarely questioned. That's why they're thoughtlessly accepted and rarely challenged. Talk about insidious! These fear-based beliefs creep into our lives and manifest themselves despite the fact that we've never knowingly even thought of them! They are assumptions that have attained the rigid status of fact and are unquestioningly passed down from generation to generation, growing stronger (as beliefs do) with use.

Here are some groundless, patently untrue beliefs that everyone can identify with. You must get sick before you die. We "catch" colds. Eating the wrong foods makes you fat. Wrinkles appear when you get old. Sex is bad. Insurance protects. Some diseases have no cure. Having fun is frivolous. Dignity, devotion and duty are virtues. You must always be rational and realistic. Work produces happiness. It's a dog-eat-dog world. Seriousness brings success. Play is just for children. You have to be able to defend yourself. Fifty thousand Frenchman can't be wrong. And so on. (You probably can identify strongly with some of these.)

The only defense against these lackful, destructive, mass-consciousness beliefs is a confident independence that consciously asserts wellness, invincibility, optimism, joyfulness, freedom, happiness, playfulness—and our ability to attract what we want. These consensus beliefs prey on vulnerability, which has been exaggerated by our fears and frightening isolated incidents into negative pervasive fact. To resist means becoming more of an individual, insisting on your right to be different from those 50,000 Frenchmen, to stay free of what happens to others—even to everyone around you.

Knowing how the Universe works breaks the grip of mass-consciousness if you continually apply it. Because you alone create all that comes to you, intend awareness of those hidden assumptions in your own belief system. Confidently and deliberately create what you want by expecting your dreams to come true. Genuinely expect, and you can be or do or have anything.

Now let's test your ability to put the Law of Attraction to work. Decide that this experiment is going to be fun and easy. (Working hard at creating rarely works.) You're going to create a hard-to-find parking space right where you want it. All you need is a crowded parking lot that you can visualize—ideally a place you commute to every day. Drive to the lot relaxed (maybe chatting or listening to music). As you approach the lot (but still out of sight of it), mentally picture the area you want to park in. Then picture an empty slot waiting just for you. Don't put extra pressure on yourself by making it a specific slot.

When you see it in your mind, smile and nod to help generate the needed positive expectation emotionally. Believe that it's waiting. Decide another car just left it. Expect it. With childlike innocence, remind yourself that you can have anything you want. Shrug to relax your shoulders. Giggle about what you're doing. Feel good about getting a space the easy way. Enjoy your triumph as you visualize your car gliding into your custom-created space. Beam with pride. (The idea is to keep yourself positively focused and expecting success so doubt can't slip in.) Now pull into the crowded parking lot, drive to your chosen area and find your waiting space. As you park in it, laugh at your success. It's important to take credit for your creation because doing so builds confidence in your ability to create. Know that this was no accident. You did everything right, so the Universe had to deliver.

If you don't succeed the first time, it's because you tried too hard or let resistance from doubt or past frustration and failure creep in to counter your creation. Shrug it off. Forgive yourself for being rusty at childlike expectation. It's a long time since you deliberately created anything. Don't get down on yourself. Be patient and forgiving. You can try again tomorrow.

Shift your attention to the next happy event in your day, something you're really looking forward to. You can clear the air by forcefully declaring that All is Well. It really is. Look around for something to appreciate. It will shift your mood. Remind yourself that nothing is more important than Feeling Good. Smile. Smiling, says science, actually breaks the grip of negativity and generates good feeling. And laughing exercises every cell in your body, energizing you and generating good feeling. So let it happen. Laughing breaks depression and lifts your mood. If you can't find something funny to laugh at, try laughing at your serious self!

Dream up other minor miracles you'd like to create. Remember, you have to be able to honestly expect success, so pick desires you believe you can create—without a lot of doubt or other forms of resistance. Or if initial failure won't dissuade you, aim for higher, bigger creations, for things or events where your desire is super-strong. Huge desire can replace expectation in overcoming resistance.

There you have it—Creation in a nutshell. You now have all the tools you need to create anything and everything you want. Remember, you can be or do or have anything you can imagine, desire or expect. No limits.

The groundwork has now been laid for learning to control every aspect of your life—including your death. Now that you know how things actually work, it will be easier to die peacefully and easily when you want. In the next two chapters, the experts will show you how.

~

"Why fear death? Death is only a beautiful adventure."

–WALT WHITMAN

"The life of a soul on earth lasts beyond his departure."

–ANGELO PATRI

7

DIE WHEN YOU CHOOSE

The foundation has been laid. The experts have explained how the Universe works. We know that the creation of anything and everything is entirely in our hands—or rather in our thoughts and emotions. We've learned there are no such things as accident, fate, luck or chance. We attract every event in our life with our thoughts—including our death. But death, as we shall see, requires a prior decision to die. We can't die, it turns out, until we decide to. Once we choose death, we begin to attract it. Every death—no matter the circumstances—requires the decision to end this lifetime. No exceptions!

This chapter will set the stage for you to take complete control of the circumstances of your death, to die when and how YOU want, not how and when society dictates.

My hope is to help the experts from the other side help you understand the following: (1) Death is always a choice, with no exceptions. You can't die until you make the decision to depart! (2) You can therefore consciously, deliberately decide the time and circumstance of your death. (3) You don't have to be terminally ill, decrepit or incapacitated to die. You don't even have to be sick—or old! That's a radical revelation, but true. It's all your choice.

Speaking from the experience of innumerable deaths, our experts assure us that death is just one more choice, the final one of this lifetime. They often say they wish they hadn't waited so long to decide to pass over, because it turned out that death was nothing to fear after all. And the afterlife turned out to be something to look forward to, because it's so pleasant. So you don't have to let others dictate when and how you die. You now have a better option.

There is remarkable unanimity among the experts from the other side on two points: (1) There is no death; and (2) Death is always a choice. That sounds contradictory, but it isn't. These statements simply involve two different definitions of death, theirs and ours, apples and oranges; it's a matter of semantics. The word death in, "There is no death," represents enlightened universal knowledge, while the death in, "Death is a choice," uses our limited earthly view of the expiration of our body and the end of this lifetime. Here the experts are speaking on our terms in order to help us understand that what we think of as "the end" really isn't. Furthermore, they explain, death is within our control, so we needn't feel the helplessness that leads to the nine fears listed in Chapter 3.

From the enlightened, vastly experienced perspective, there is no death because there is no ending, only a transformation or transition. We now know that modern quantum physicists heartily agree. What we call death the experts—plus the enlightened and physicists—consider merely a rebirth into the non-physical realm. To them, death of the body is no big deal because, thanks to their experience, they see beyond it to an unending series of lifetimes joyfully separated by delicious interludes in the non-physical realm. They know they cannot die, and they view non-physical existence as something to look forward to, a fresh beginning, not nothingness or the end or the unknown. Death therefore isn't something to dread. Just the opposite! To us it seems to be the end because we can't see beyond it. They're trying to erase our fears by giving us the benefit of their vast experience with the endless cycle of life and death—or more accurately: physical life, non-physical; physical, non-physical—for eternity.

Because the experts know from experience that death is always a choice, they state that "Every death is a suicide." In this radical statement they use our crude dictionary definitions of death and suicide: i.e., "The taking of one's own life voluntarily, deliberate self-inflicted death—doing yourself in." But they know it's only the death of the body.

LETTING GO

For purposes of this discussion, I more explicitly define suicide as deliberately "killing the physical body to end life." The definition is the same for physician-assisted death. The deliberate releasing of the soul that the experts are trying to teach us, while technically suicide, I call "Letting Go" to distinguish it from earthly suicide. Letting Go does not require damaging the body, much less incapacitating it so severely that the heart stops beating. Committing suicide is always violent, crude, traumatic, ignorant, purely physical and unnecessary, leading to a difficult joyless transition to non-physical. By contrast, Letting Go is gentle, enlightened, spiritual, peaceful and free, ensuring an easy and ecstatic transition to a delightful afterlife. So why not take the easy way out?

TWO KINDS OF DEATH CHOICE

The prerequisite for dying is the decision to let go of life. But there are two different kinds of choice: conscious and unconscious. The difference between them is huge. The vast majority of people die after making an unconscious choice to give up on life and accept death. Unconscious death is totally without individual conscious control. It's usually put off as long as possible, and accompanied by fear and suffering, degeneration and terminal illness. Its circumstances are usually dictated by the subject's acceptance of society's rigid, inhuman, insane requirements for a miserably "proper" death. Plus the fear and feelings of unworthiness and incompleteness which prolong life.

Conscious dying means deliberate, controlled death. Included are suicides and assisted deaths, which require violently killing the body. Far more civilized, dignified and humane is Letting Go, which is the peaceful release of the personality and soul. If you want to know more about euthanasia (i.e., well-planned assisted suicide), consult books such as *Final Exit* by Derek Humphry, or get in touch with the Hemlock Society. Conscious dying is above all deliberate. Its circumstances should fit the person's intent, attitude, desires and beliefs.

My intent is to help the experts teach you to die consciously, NOT by killing your body, but by deliberately and peacefully Letting Go of the essential timeless you when you wish.

SETH SPEAKS

Now let's hear what the renowned spiritual teacher Seth, trusted counselor to tens of thousands over a period of four decades, has to say about death and the necessity of choosing it, just as we choose everything else in life. Seth teaches that we cannot die by accident. Because the Law of Attraction has no exceptions, and because we create with our thoughts, accidents—the frequently cited cause of death—cannot exist. Like luck, and chance, there's no room for accident in the equation of creation. Seth says, "No one dies under any circumstances who is not prepared to die." So neither natural catastrophe, nor muggers, nor head-on collisions kill anyone who isn't ready to die. The Universe arranges that only people who are ready to die are waiting in the path of what we call accidents.

Death is always a choice, not always clear-cut or dramatic or decisive or even conscious, but a choice nevertheless. You make that choice and the Universe does the rest. You need not be suicidal or actively seeking death to decide to let go of life. Seth explains that you might die simply because you hold "a lesser claim to life," e.g., you might hold the attitude, "I will live or die as the fates decide." You might get on a plane destined to crash, while those with a strong desire to live will not be aboard. "People who have come close to accepting the idea of dying might choose actions or lifestyles that willingly risk death."

"The decision to die," says Seth, "may simply be the absence of a vital, personal, direct affirmative intent to live. Each of us is born out of a desire to live this lifetime and dies when that desire fades and dies. Active desire for death is perfectly natural, not morbid, neurotic or cowardly. It's healthy and positive to want to leave this physical life of yours when desire wanes. The time must come when you are ready for a different reality. Suicide, however, is deliberate, violent self-killing of the body, and not part of your intentions on coming into this lifetime."

Your attitude when you choose to leave this world dictates the when and how of your death. Many people attempt to make some kind of statement with their deaths. For instance, some choose natural calamities: being crushed in earthquakes, drowning in raging seas, being blown away in hurricanes, falling off mountains—for the high-energy drama and bravery associated with that kind of death. Seth says, "Each person caught by an epidemic or natural disaster had private reasons for choosing thus to die."

Some may decide to die protesting in riots to prove their dedication to a cause, but the experts say we die for a cause only when we've found no cause to live by! "Death is the final chance to make a meaningful statement—for those who fear they have failed to make their beliefs known."

Increasing numbers of youth die young. Seth says, "Some fear old age will bring an unendurable degradation of both the spirit and the body. Many of them—idealists—choose death because they fear life could never bring the fulfillment they yearn for. For them, death with drama seems preferable to living. The powerless, with no hope, often come together (as at Jonestown) to make an even bigger statement with group death. Often these people feel physical life has failed them."

Older adults often choose a long-suffering martyrdom in the hospital. Many are too worn out or have no need to make a statement to the world. Death from sudden illness or in a wartime battle—it's all choice. "Cancer," says Seth, "is a disease contracted by people who want to die but are ashamed to admit it because they fear that seeking death would be condemned as insane when most of the species is struggling to stay alive. The variations in death choices and death wishes are as endless as the people who create them.

"We're born instinctively knowing that death is not the end, only a transformation of consciousness." In childhood we somehow know that we're immortal. As adults we yearn to recover that belief, hoping that death is not the end, that we are going to survive it. Those who identify life solely with the body tend to believe that death is the end. Those in touch with their emotions and spirit are more likely to expect that there's life after death. Death is as much a creation as birth. We're told the body is aware of its eventual death, even at birth. Each individual, we're told, unconsciously knows the time of his death. Most people also are aware of a desire for death after they've made the necessary decision—but again the awareness is usually unconscious.

Seth says, "Each of us comes here with a particular agenda for this lifetime. The child who dies young probably came back just to experience childhood. And it probably chose parents who could accept that intent through mutual attraction. The young often choose dramatic exits with strong messages. Many identify with wild powerful nature. Nature and man work together. Some people feel it imperative to die physically to assure that they survive spiritually and psychically. So do not grieve their loss, only your own. Remember, all deaths are suicides. People die when they are ready, and never without their own reasons."

NDEs CONFIRM DEATH IS A CHOICE

Probably the strongest evidence supporting the contention that you can't die until you decide to comes not from the dead but from "those who should have died but didn't," right here in the flesh-and-blood physical world. These are the thousands of people walking among us who have died and come back to life to tell us what it was like— at least its early stages. Near Death Experiences (NDEs) have been repeatedly collected, studied and compared by researchers. And there's remarkable consensus about what the early stages of death are like. In Chapter 8 we'll look more closely at a summary of hundreds of NDEs to compare it with what the experts from the other side tell us about what to expect from death and the hereafter.

The aspect of NDEs we're looking at here is the subject's stubborn refusal to die when they should have, apparently because they hadn't made the necessary choice. They were too full of life. They just weren't ready to go. Their "number wasn't up." Their time had not yet come. They weren't through living. The best-known source of NDE data is from Raymond Moody, M.D., author of *Life After Life*, a 1975 book that has sold some three million copies. The 150 NDE subjects he interviewed were either (1) resuscitated after being judged clinically dead, (2) suffered accidents, illness or severe injury that brought them to the brink of physical death, or (3) people who managed to relate to others what was happening as they died.

Details differed, but the core experience of death was remarkably consistent. The most remarkable aspect of these accounts is that each person "survived to tell the tale," survived an experience that would have killed most people.

While Moody did not specifically investigate the mental health, expectations and intents of his subjects, he describes them as "basically strong personalities who weren't through living; functional and well balanced, certain of the reality of what they experienced." In fact they said their NDE was more intense and real than anything they'd ever experienced in life! Clearly they hadn't made the decision to die, and so they didn't. Instead, they survived experiences that should have killed them and then returned to good health and renewed zestful life. Why? Apparently because they hadn't even thought about death, much less invited it.

Many of the subjects testified that they didn't want to die and successfully strived to return to their bodies, especially those in the early moments of death, because they had strong feelings about unfinished business in this lifetime. There was more they wanted, remaining purpose in their lives. But many other NDEs found the afterlife so wonderful and free on the other side that they badly wanted to remain, to enjoy the relief and strange, wonderful new feelings. It didn't matter. They came back to life, because they hadn't decided to die.

It's interesting to note that typical Moody subjects reported that their NDEs radically changed their view of the relationship of life and death, releasing a lifetime of fear, profoundly altering their lives for the better, allowing them to lead happier healthier lives. Typically, they say, it taught them the importance of love as well as life and gave them renewed determination to reach new goals. They variously likened the NDE to a homecoming reunion with deceased relatives, an awakening from a lovely dream, a proud happy graduation, and getting out of jail. Because they encountered nothing remotely resembling hell (or a validation of karma), they were able to let go of religious beliefs that painted a controlling, reward-punishment view of the afterlife.

Humanity has been tormented since the dawn of man by the question, "What is it like to die?" NDEs probably come closest—in the physical world—to giving us a glimpse of what is waiting for us on the other side.

ABRAHAM SPEAKS

The non-physical entity Abraham shows us how much our lives are shaped not by our desires but what we think will bring approval from others—or at least avoid the shame that brings strong feelings of guilt. "Release your desire for approval," they exhort. "You will always be out of balance if you care how others feel, because they all want something different from you. Don't look over your shoulder to see what others, individuals and society (mass consciousness) advise, before you act." Trying to please everyone can tear you apart.

Nowhere is the influence of others more pathetically obvious and destructive than as death approaches. "Most of your illness," Abraham says, "comes from confusion and fear regarding living and dying. You're so convinced that you must prove yourselves worthy of something that you're afraid to die, afraid you've failed to qualify, fearing you're not finished, haven't accomplished enough by society's standards. You therefore unconsciously decide to protect yourself from shame and guilt by triggering a natural-appearing bodily decline—illness or decrepitude—to give yourself an acceptable excuse to depart. It seems the only logical way out because you've been brainwashed to believe it's improper to go any other way."

This shocking indictment of our view of death and our sad need for approval from others reveals the awful power of two forces that shape the quality of our lives and direct us toward miserable frightened deaths (and lives). We pay a terrible price to dodge the "shame and guilt" we fear will descend upon us if we fail to follow the prescriptions of an ignorant society.

Abraham continues by urging, "Don't dread death. Embrace life and All That Is. There is only eternal life and joy. When you realize that, you'll stop pushing against death and your now will become as full as you intended it to be. You're an extension of the universe, not a separate entity. You're a conscious creator forever. You're not here to prove anything to anybody. You're here because it's the perfect place to get the exaggerated contrast that this physical environment provides. Here it's easier to see what's wanted and what's not. That's why you came back: to make choices about what's created, to add to All That Is.

"Society hints that you have some grand purpose in

this lifetime. Unfortunately, earthly reports of that purpose are often conflicting and grandiose, with cunningly concealed agendas that often involve serving others or their beliefs. Few of you realize that you're merely here to reconnect with your Inner Beings, to grow, to have fun, to become more than you were, to aid evolution. So try to resist fear. Fear of any kind sabotages life. Fear is attention, so it actually attracts what's feared! Tell yourself, 'I'm an eternal being. There is no ending to who I am. When I'm physical I can focus sharply on specific experiences. When I'm non-physical I bask in that fuller broader perspective.'

"The death of the young and/or healthy is always a great shock to society, making it ask, 'What went wrong?' It thinks there has to be a fatal accident or illness to explain it. Then it's okay. Society doesn't understand that every death was preceded by a decision to die, even among the young and the healthy. So stop worrying about death. It doesn't exist. Life is eternal. To avoid deterioration and disease, remind yourself, 'I am the creator of all my experience. I attract everything that happens to me.' Above all, don't mimic the unwanted actions you see in others. You don't have to get sick or age just because others do. Remember, each of you are individual creators. Give your attention only to that which you admire in others and in society. To live to whatever age you want, try to find your balanced place of joy, and stay there. The trick is think joy, not pleasing others."

SIX MISTAKEN BELIEFS ABOUT DEATH

Abraham continues, "Your bad feelings about death come from your mistaken beliefs that, (1) We're in this lifetime to prove ourselves worthy of something. (2) We haven't done it yet. (3) We have only one life to live, so we have to get it right. (4) We feel inadequate. (5) We fear anything unknown. (6) We fear an absolute ending, followed by nothingness. Use this checklist to test your beliefs. If any of these are yours, you need to exchange them for some of the following.

"Here's how you counter those feelings of unworthiness and avoid the pressure of mass consciousness, the media and society, so you can die in peace. (1) Don't try so hard to figure everything out at once. (2) Pay better attention to your guidance system, letting your feelings direct your actions. (3) Be easier on yourself, less demanding. (4) Go slower. (5) Look for your own positive aspects. (6) Look for them in others. These steps will allow you to attract more of what you want, counteracting the unworthy feelings that go on and on and keep you alive but in misery beyond your time.

"What's the prescription for a perfect death? Acknowledge that there is no death, only everlasting life. When you recognize that you have gleaned all you wanted from this physical lifetime, decide you are ready to re-emerge into non-physical. Say to yourself, 'I now want to return to my fuller broader non-physical perspective.' Then you will easily release yourself from your body. You'll find it's better than jumping off a tall building or stepping in front of a speeding car or drinking yourself to death.

"Getting sick before you die is really pointless," continues Abraham, shifting gears. "It's a waste of life, not to mention unpleasant. The majority of you think you have to get sick because you dread death and you're pushing hard against it. Worrying about death makes you pinch off your stream of life-giving energy, literally choking out life. You can't allow life and push against death at the same time! You use worry as your excuse to make yourself sick enough to die the way society wants, when life could be far more pleasant right up until you decide it's time to go. When you're ready, go quickly and easily.

"Death isn't a bad thing, just inevitable. It's not worth getting sick over. You're only sick because you hold thoughts that contradict your desire for perfect health. Mass-consciousness negative thought forms grow huge and powerful when they are fueled by fear of death, fear of society's wrath and the expectation of sickness. Put your attention on healthy people who live as they please and let them be your example. Refuse to give attention to anything negative—like fearful angry people, TV, newspapers, radio, disastrous events and your own worrisome thoughts. They have nothing to do with you if they don't match your desire. The trick is to want so much to feel good that you won't let negativity in. Then you won't get sick. And you won't need to get sick in order to die.

DIE IN YOUR PRIME

"Be in your prime on the day you die," Abraham goes on. "You are born into a culture that feels guilty about dying—a place with laughably strict laws regulating the end of life. But ironically, in the end, you all make the decision to die, without exception. You are all committing suicide when you go! So you're all guilty of breaking the law! You may attract physical evidence that your death is somebody else's fault, but there are no accidents. You die by choice, whether it's deliberate or by default. Your life and your decision bring it about.

"What you don't realize is that it was never your intention to live a long life. There's no point in living when your capacity is diminished. After you lose your focus and your vitality, you can no longer accomplish what you came for. You get most of your work done early in life. You came forth with a relatively short life span in mind, but society makes you feel so guilty about leaving that, at an early age, you adopt the strange and unnecessary belief that a physical decline must precede death—because you feel you need justification to die! You feel you can't leave in good grace unless something BAD happens to you first. You think you have to get sick, decrepit or run over by a truck to have the excuse you need to excuse yourself. That's the source of your belief in illness and degeneration!

"It's at the root of your feelings of vulnerability, an inherent, entrenched part of your overall perspective. What nonsense! It's okay to stay in physical—or not—as you please. So do as you please. You can live in your prime, like the old wolf, until the day you die. You don't *have* to get weak or sick or run over. Stay in this lifetime for 20 years or 100, but only stay as long as you really *want* to. Love your healthy energetic body right to the end. Reject all negative focus of attention. Don't go looking for an excuse to leave that's acceptable to society. That's not a requirement for dying. It's only a belief, and you can change beliefs. Remember, you can and will decide when and how you die. So why not choose circumstances that fit your desires?

"When you stop wanting to live, it's okay to die. But it's foolish to cling to life when you'd rather die and move on. You don't have to accomplish everything in this lifetime. Don't forget, you're coming back. So, when life gets too hard, when you've lost your adventurous edge, your zest and vigor and passion, thanks to the pressure of mass-consciousness, aging and illness—just let go. You can come back fresh, so why stay and work too hard? When you decided to be reborn, it was your broad intent to seek a new perspective. A short lifetime is sufficient for the experience you seek, while there's vigor, energy and appetite.

"When the energy of the universe is streaming through you, you're a deliberate creator and life is wonderful. You don't want to die. When you've grown weary and have disconnected from the positive stream of life-giving energy, you die. Remember, death is not an ending, just a shift in focus from physical to non-physical. Non-physical is the more dominant of the two, because you have your memory and the wisdom of the ages at your fingertips and are closer to the universal source. So don't be intimidated by your society into living longer than you truly desire. It's the quality of your life that counts, not its length. Long years are no virtue.

"Many people, later in life, judge that this world is just too tough and decide they don't want to come back for another lifetime, but that's just the physical talking. Non-physical is wonderful, but in time we all want to come back for fresh experience. Physical perspective is severely limited, but it offers stimulating experience and contrast that can't be obtained elsewhere.

"Eastern religions have as a goal an escape from what they see as a treadmill of repeated lifetimes. It's a status thing because there's a stigma attached to 'having to come back.' They see it as a 'failure to ascend.' They think they have to stop the cycle in order to bask in non-physical enlightenment, but that's because they don't understand that they already have full control. They don't realize they can be or do or have whatever they want now. And they can't conceive that their viewpoint, once they're in non-physical, will extend far beyond their present knowing and will be utterly different than they imagine. Despite their present intentions and hopes, they'll be back."

EVENTUALLY YOU CROAK!

Abraham continues: "Pushing against death—fearing it, fearing your departure—compromises life, reducing its quality. Death is simply the result of not letting the stream of energy from the universe flow through you. You increasingly get tired and cranky, more resistant to change and slower. And eventually you 'croak.' We use that disrespectful term to shock you, because from our broader view death doesn't exist. Life goes on, there is no death, only a transition, a shift, a change of focus, a transformation.

"Death is a minor milestone, no big deal. Instead of fearing it and fighting it, worrying yourself sick over it, you ought to look forward to its delicious relief, its new beginning, its fresh adventure. Say to yourself, 'This life has been great. I've done everything I could imagine or wanted to do here. I wonder what comes next.' Then turn eagerly to what lies just around the corner.

"Live in the now. That's what the beasts do. Creatures of every kind recognize when they're about to become a bigger creature's lunch. They don't struggle or suffer. They just relax into that blissful knowing. They knew what the end would be before they came. They live in the now. They're good at it, and they don't push against anything. So they easily make the transition from physical to non-physical without missing a beat. That's the optimum way to go for humans, too. Instead of desperately resisting death, go easily, peacefully.

"A young mother who was dying might worry about leaving her little children behind, feeling she hadn't done her job, hadn't met her responsibilities. On her death bed she might agonize, 'What will they do without me?' But that's just society's mass-consciousness view of the situation. There are other possibilities. And this is no accident. When she re-emerges into non-physical she will immediately recognize her children as the powerful beings they are, and see that they are here to live their own life experience. That experience will surely include her death at an early age. It may be just what's needed to teach them to grow and prosper. So she needn't agonize and despair. All is well.

"Your broad intent coming into this lifetime was, 'Let me go forth and I will live the fullest that I can live for as long as it feels good, then I will return.' Unfortunately, as your lifetime unfolds you may be seduced by society's negative perspectives. Your beliefs and fears may change your original intent, giving you a new decision regarding death. Often you give up that 'living as long as it feels good' intent to comply with your culture's urging to live as long as you can, no matter what.

"Your society has laughable, but often tragic, beliefs about when and how we ought to die that have become ridiculously rigid, hardening into Right and Wrong. But they are only beliefs and they are contradicted by the wisdom from the other side."

INSIGHTS ON DEATH

I find it fascinating, when I hear of the death of a celebrity or someone I know, to remember that there are no accidents; every death is by choice. So I know that person died because he or she wanted to die or was through with life. It provides a rare insight into their thinking and feel-ings, especially when that person was young or healthy or seemed to have had a happy, even enviable, life—to know that deep down they were ready to die—or at least had lost the will to live. Fascinating!

For example, Abraham explains the inner circum-stances and feelings surrounding the recent death of Prin-cess Diana and her boyfriend Dodi, viewed by the world as a major tragedy. "Princess Di," says Abraham, "had long ago allowed her desire to live to decline. She knew she could never have the peace and privacy she yearned for. She had all but stopped hoping for them, becoming re-signed to the heavy limitations of her fame and celebrity. When she fell in love with Dodi, their desire for privacy rose sharply to new heights, but their expectation of achiev-ing it sunk to new lows. This disparity made them with-draw further from the public eye and increased their re-sentment of intrusion.

"The strong conflict between their desires and their expectations produced massive resistance. Their anger and frustration and helplessness and futility made them mag-nets for death, fiercely attracting it. By pushing furiously against life they invited death. The situation became un-endurable for them, destroying their appetites for life. This overpowering negative emotion became so high that the only escape from it was to leave this physical lifetime. All the criteria for passing had been met. All the players played their parts, and the result was inevitable: early death. It was a perfect example of the workings of the universe.

"It was the same for Mother Theresa. Her desire for life had declined to the point that she was ready to die, and so she did, according to the laws of the universe. It was a similar 'no escape' situation. The worldwide outpouring of grief over these deaths showed your society's great desire to understand death. These deaths raised feelings of vulnerability and shook the mistaken belief that death must be viewed as bad. These deaths of prominent people may help explain how the loss of will to live becomes a willingness to die and constitutes the choice that begins to attract the circumstances of death."

MANY JUST "LET GO"

Statisticians tell us that elderly broken-hearted spouses who have lost their loved ones and men who have retired after a long career—only live another 16-18 months. Their jobs and close companions sustained their strong interest in life. Without that stimulus a steep decline in the will to live apparently sets in. Unable to find stimulating substitutes, they lose interest in life and make the shift toward death that soon attracts it.

There is ample evidence in this world, if you look for it, that many thousands of people have used their ability to choose death to die suddenly and deliberately and without apparent cause. In prison camps and during torture there are recorded accounts of soldiers suddenly willing themselves to die. Arizona Senator Barry Goldwater, who had frequently stated that he would decide the time and circumstances of his death, appears to have done just that. He died peacefully in his home, surrounded by family. His wife Susan said, "It is the family's firm belief that he decided the moment of his death. He made up his mind with courage and enormous dignity. He closed his eyes and soared."

All of us without exception make the choice to die, but it's often an unconscious decision. What the experts are trying to tell us is that we can take full control of our death, making its time and circumstances fit our beliefs and desires, by making our decision conscious and deliberate. We can simply Let Go when and how we want, not just by default when it's next to impossible to remain and too late to do anything else.

There's a laughable but deeply ingrained western cultural adage that insists, "Everyone has to die of *some*thing." Native Americans, however, frequently appear to die of nothing at all, quietly defying this popular societal belief. Their upbringing didn't include that limiting teaching. So when the circumstances fit, their spirits are released and they go off to join their ancestors. Their shamanistic beliefs have taught them that they can Let Go their spirits whenever they are ready. And so they do. You can too!

Abraham tells the story of a southern gentleman who had always been healthy, happy and independent well into old age, refusing to be sick or miserable. But his feisty stubborn independence brought him increasing disapproval. One day he slipped and fell, injuring his hip. The injury wasn't life-threatening but it made him think. The next day he told his grandson, "I'll be with the Lord tonight." Sure enough, he died peacefully in his sleep.

Abraham explains that, "Unlike most people, he did not make his transition because he had to. He was not unhappy. But he was getting tired of society hammering away at him. When the criticism got to him he got to thinking about what might come next and started joyously moving toward it, bringing forth the decision to move on. That attracted the fall, which he recognized immediately as an omen. He decided the time had come, consciously deciding to go to sleep that night for the final time, knowing he would wake up in a better place."

A great many mysterious but peaceful deaths, which the coroner variously reports as "unexplained," "natural causes" or "heart failures," are probably the result of people who discover they can consciously Let Go when they want to or desperately need to end their suffering. There's no way to know—here in the physical world. In non-physical, however, everybody knows that it's only a small proportion of the total. That's why they're trying to help us—because Letting Go is the easy way out. They say our crazy irrational beliefs about death, not death itself, are responsible for our fears. Those beliefs are wrong in almost every way possible! Death is something to look forward to when this life is through, not something to dread!

CONSCIOUS DYING

Eastern religions, while subject to the same drawbacks

as those in the West (i.e., all religions seek to control) are firmly grounded in the belief in reincarnation and eternal life. Furthermore, there is strong belief in the merits of conscious dying. So it's not surprising that holy men in the East spend a lot of time learning how to die properly. In a book titled *Graceful Exits: How Great Beings Die* (Death Stories of 108 Tibetan, Hindu and Zen Masters), most ac.... ints show that disciples were informed in advance when and how their masters would depart.

Some took pride in dying sitting or standing; one man climbed in his coffin and promptly stopped breathing. Some were not ill, or even old. Others were over a hundred. At the time of death there was always pain-free peace and serenity. Some died smiling, or singing or laughing. Most instructed their disciples not to grieve. "It is not the end," they explained. "I will rise again." They died when they felt their work in this lifetime was done. Typical attitudes at death were joy, fearlessness, courage, cheerfulness, simplicity and humility. The consensus wish was to identify with the Inner Being, soul or essence before leaving their bodies.

"Leave this life like an eagle soaring up into the blue sky," one advised. Another (Guru Nanak) reminded that "Death is but a gateway to birth." "Strive for a readiness to die," wrote Milarepa. "Be certain and ready when the time comes. You will have no fear and no regret." Ramakrishna wrote, "The body was born and it will die. But for the soul there is no death. The body and the soul are two different things." Other wise men explained that, "To die is merely to rest...Death is only sleep...Death is not death but liberation."

Well-known celebrity psychic Kevin Ryerson channels an entity named John who corroborates everything we've heard from Abraham and Seth. "There is no death," John reiterates. "Only the passing from one plane to another. Loss of the body is like shedding an old garment. Have no fear of stepping lightly from one lifetime to the next. Death is part of the natural cycle of life. You are a being composed of mind, body and spirit. The physical body is but a single part of your true nature."

Now let's hear from another eminent expert from the other side. Ramtha describes himself as a "sovereign entity who lived a long time on earth (and is) now part of an unseen brotherhood that loves mankind greatly—here to remind you of a heritage you forgot long ago." He explains that, "Death is only the ending of the body, not the personality-self that lives within it. It is the attitudes of this personality-self that degrade the life-force and evoke death. The body is only a servant, without a mind of its own. It can only respond to what it is told to do. Your soul, under the direction of your attitudes and thoughts, causes certain hormones to be dispensed throughout the body in order to maintain life.

"Because of your negative attitudes, those hormones cease to be created after puberty. Their absence activates a death hormone that begins to break down the body and cause it to grow old and to die. The death hormone is activated by guilt and self-judgement and the fear of death. You anticipate death by buying insurance to bury yourself and to protect your treasury. You do everything possible to hasten aging and bodily death—because you wholly expect it. You accept thoughts of old age and expect the body to wither away and die."

SECRETS OF GROWING YOUNGER

Ramtha continues, "You have the power within you to reverse the aging of your body back into youth. If you don't want the body to age, change your attitude. Say to yourself that the body will live forever and it will. Remove the word 'old' from your vocabulary. Replace it with 'forever.' Cease celebrating birthdays for they give credence to the aging process. Reverse the count of your years and become younger. Always live in the present. Never acknowledge any future beyond this now. Contemplate the foreverness of your body, not how long you might live. Love yourself, bless your body and command it to bring forth the enzymes of youth, and it will."

HISTORICAL PRECEDENTS

Ancient writings reveal that conscious dying has been around since the dawn of civilization. Though foreign to Westerners, the concept is at least 6,000 years old. Plato wrote, "Every soul...is ordained to wander between incarnations..." In India it was written in the Sixth Century that "The self does not die when the body dies." Ancient mythological and scriptural writings speak of the same sequence of events at death that were noted by those subjects in Dr. Moody's NDE book. Buddha, Pythagoras, the Mystery Schools of Egypt, Greece, Rome, Persia and China, all believed in reincarnation and conscious dying.

The Tibetan and Egyptian *Books of the Dead* echo the experiences of NDEs and give careful instruction in conscious dying. And there have been dozens of other guidebooks down the centuries for how to consciously meet death. It must be remembered, however, that the Hindus and Buddhists believe that one's final thoughts, at the moment of death, determine the character of the next incarnation (lifetime), and their aim is to awaken in a more enlightened incarnation. They strive for the same kind of control over the time and circumstances of their death that I call Letting Go.

Christ and early Christian sects believed in reincarnation, and such beliefs can be found in the New Testament Bible. In Matthew 17:13, Christ says John the Baptist is actually an incarnation of the prophet Elijah.

THERE'S NO NEED TO GRIEVE

Abraham says, "When you realize that everyone who dies—whether they were killed in war, got run over by a steamroller, or died of cancer—did so by choice, it makes little sense to mourn for them. They not only chose to die— or turned their backs on life—they also chose the time and circumstances of their death. Their dying was just as intentional as if it was suicide, because in a way it was. It may have been less conscious and less deliberate than suicide or euthanasia, but it was choice just the same. For whatever reasons, they were ready to re-emerge into the pot of well-being. So don't grieve for their untimely death. Don't assume that something went terribly wrong. It didn't.

"In your society, grieving is seen as normal, even obligatory. You're supposed to give up having fun and act grave, wear black and cry just because somebody died. Big deal. Everybody has to die, so why all the fuss? Dying's normal. Grieving doesn't help them and isn't good for you. It disconnects you from the source of life energy—the same disconnection that leads to death. Grieving is purely negative. Stay negative long enough and your Guidance System accepts your negativity as normal and doesn't warn you anymore. When feeling bad becomes normal, you're on the long slide toward disease and death. So don't grieve for those who die. They're where they want to be. Don't feel sorry for them, they're probably happier than you are!"

That's what the experts have to say about death and the hereafter. If you're still strongly beset with many of the nine fears enumerated in Chapter 3—plus perhaps a fear of Hell or karma—it's unlikely that you'll exercise control over your death. But if you can think of death—as I do—as wonderful relief from all your pains and cares, a fresh beginning, a new adventure, a reunion with friends and family, an altogether delightful, enlightening experience, then perhaps you'll be unwilling to hang on to this lifetime with a death grip until you can't stand it any longer, or your physical apparatus flat out refuses to continue.

Personally, I look forward to a joyful, easy transition to the afterlife when I tire of this lifetime—never mind what anybody else thinks. How to make that easy transition is the exciting subject of Chapter 8.

~

"Brief as falling water will be death."

–CONRAD AIKEN

"How wonderful is death."

–SHELLEY

8

HOW TO "LET GO"... AND WHAT COMES NEXT!

The stage is now set. Here comes the payoff. This chapter will show you how to peacefully part from your body in style, when and how you want. It will also tell you what to expect from the transition we call death, and set forth the delights of the afterlife that awaits. You'll find that death can actually be something to look forward to—not the horror you've probably been taught to fear.

In Chapter 7 you learned that every death requires the decision to die—or at least a willingness to let go of life. So every death is technically suicide. You can't die until you decide to. Once the critical decision is made, you begin to attract the sort of death that fits your current attitudes and beliefs. The decision to die is usually unconscious, so the circumstances of your death—thanks to society-dictated attitudes and beliefs—will often be far different from what you want deep down! Of course you'd like an easy, pain-free, peaceful, dignified death, but you're bucking a life-time of society's contrary teachings, and typically you're afraid of what others might think, so probably you get sick and cling to life with a death grip as long as you possibly can before fearfully, unpleasantly dying. Sad—and so unnecessary.

Fortunately, because a decision to die is required, you can make it a conscious decision for an easy peaceful—even joyful—death instead of grimly hanging on until the failure of your body forces you into an unconscious decision. These two options are worlds apart. A conscious decision allows you to take complete control of every aspect of your death. It gives you the chance to dictate a happy, peaceful, dignified passing that perfectly fits your inner-most desires—if you're strong enough to turn your back on contrary teachings, and on society's grim requirements for a proper—but miserable—death.

You don't have to be terminally ill—or even old to Let Go, because the fact is you don't owe society either a long life or a slow death. Life is not a longevity contest, to see who can last the longest, no matter what, with the winner being he who suffers the longest, ends up in the worst shape, and experiences the worst death. That's a contest you don't want to win, because the grim prize is Death American Style!

NDEs REVISITED

In Chapter 7 we saw that studies of Near Death Experiences (NDEs) showed that those experiences were remarkably consistent, and that they strongly supported the contention of our experts from the other side that every death requires the decision to let go of life. We saw evidence that people who hadn't made that decision either refused to die or came back to life after experiences that should have killed them. They simply weren't through with life. We'll take a close look at the consensus description of what a typical NDE is like in order to compare it with our experts' first-hand report of what to expect from death and the afterlife.

NDEs, you'll recall, are experiences of ordinary people who were resuscitated after being clinically dead, or who had suffered accidents or illness that brought them to the brink of death, or who managed to describe the experience to someone as they died. Many of them found the afterlife so delightful that they wanted to remain. They likened their NDE to a homecoming, awakening or graduation. But they couldn't stay because they hadn't yet made the decision to die.

Both the experts and people who have experienced an NDE insist that death is nothing like what we here on earth have been taught. For instance, we're told that you're either dead or alive, one or the other, with nothing in between. The experts and NDEs, as we shall see, agree that there's a *lot* in between! For instance, most of us think that once a person stops breathing and his heart stops beating that he's stone-cold dead, with no further awareness of this world. Not true! A corpse, it turns out, may have great awareness (sight, hearing, etc.) for another ten days! So be careful what you say in the presence of the dead. They're watching and listening! Both our experts and the NDEs agree that our earthly authorities literally don't know what they're talking about.

Clearly, NDEers come closest—in this physical world—to showing us what death, at least the early stage, is like—and what's waiting beyond it on the other side. Dr. Raymond Moody, after studying 150 NDEs, composed a composite picture of the typical Near Death Experience, which can be broken down into 15 separate elements, most but not all of which will dependably be present.

First, our typical subject hears himself pronounced dead by his doctor, and all pain and discomfort magically disappears. The relief is unimaginable. Next comes a loud ringing or buzzing as he moves rapidly but easily down a long dark tunnel toward a brilliant but peaceful light. Now he's outside his body and sees it from a distance. Gradually he becomes aware that he's wearing a new and very different body, one that can pass through walls and travel thousands of miles in seconds. He is welcomed by friends and relatives who try to help him adjust to his new surroundings. A warm loving spirit—a spirit of light—appears to help comfort him and help him review a panoramic account of the major events of his life. He finds he can read the minds and feelings of those he was involved with. Soon he senses the approach of a barrier or border that leads to the after-life.

He can go no farther because he hasn't made the decision to die. Somehow he returns to his body and this life-time, profoundly changed. He no longer fears death and rejects any reward-punishment (heaven-hell) view of the afterlife, though he may have accepted it as an unquestioned truth all his life.

Dr. Bruce Goldberg in *Peaceful Transition* provides a similar analysis of NDE research. He says the typical encounter unfolds like a dream but seems more real than anything ever experienced in life. There's a floating, disconnected sensation, a feeling of quiet calm detachment, inner peace and serenity, with no sense of time, and the sweet relief of complete freedom from all physical discomfort.

He summarizes: "The 'core' experience of an NDE includes (1) hearing loud noises very early in the death process; (2) moving through a long dark tunnel; (3) seeing a white or gold light that is separate from oneself; (4) seeing relevant religious figures like Jesus or Buddha or Moses; (5) experiencing a panoramic life review/judgement; and (6) realizing that this experience is a learning process."

This is a general model, because the death process, like life, is determined by individual choices. The subject's attitudes and beliefs at death strongly influence his passage. What you expect to experience at death is largely what you initially get—before beginning the above core experience.

Kenneth Ring in *Life At Death*, reports that 48% of the NDE subjects he interviewed described the above core experience. Prior religious beliefs had no influence on their Near Death Experience, only on who they would initially see. None of Ring's subjects experienced anything hellish, and 80% of them reported that after their NDE they had little or no fear of death.

After an NDE, death tends to be seen as an expanding beyond oneself, a gradual—not abrupt—passage between the physical and non-physical worlds, a slow peaceful change like snow melting in spring. It's the movement of the soul from one level of consciousness to another. The white light—brilliant but peaceful—is the principal focus of awareness during this transition. One is conscious of both the world left behind and the non-physical one just entered. How long the transition takes depends on the spiritual evolution of the soul in question and its willingness to accept—not fight—this journey from physical to non-physical. "As ye sow, so shall ye reap." There's a karma of sorts acting during transition, but even the stingiest, angriest soul, once it has accepted its new surroundings will find peace and contentment in the non-physical realm.

THE VIEW FROM BEYOND

We've heard what the early stages of death and the afterlife are like from those NDEers who have died and come back to walk among us. Now let's listen to several separate entities from beyond who have experienced death innumerable times, have intact memories of all their many lifetimes, and currently reside in the non-physical realm. John, channeled by Kenneth Ryerson whom we met in Chapter 7, tells us the first thing to understand is that there is no death, only the passing from one plane to another—like the shedding of an old garment.

To truly understand death we must realize that we consist of body, mind and spirit. At passing, the body parts from the mind and spirit. We are moving away from physical time and space toward ever-increasing consciousness. As our mind expands, our memory returns and we regain awareness of, not just this last lifetime, but of all our past lives. We see that this death is just part of a natural cycle, a single event in everlasting life. When we resist and fail to accept death, we make ourselves less than who we truly are. When we begin to understand ourselves as spirit or soul, and that our personality is just an expression of that soul, we enter into a greater life, stepping easily from one life into the next.

John tells us from personal experience, that at the moment of passing there is a greater and greater illumination that seems to fill the room. Those around us slowly dissolve and merge into a single pattern of light. The aura of each becomes illuminated. We pass through a review of the major events of our lives, then through the highlights of our past lives. Forgiveness of earthly companions becomes easier once we are illuminated, not just because we no longer have to deal with them but because we come to realize that as we forgive we are in turn forgiven. Our state of awareness grows steadily as more and more is revealed to us. There is a shutting down of earthly energy, a sense of coolness and quiet.

After this period of orientation, during which we still have contact with the earth plane, we pass along a great swirling vortex of light as our minds continually expand and memory returns, on our way to a higher order of celestial beings, eventually to become one with God. On the way, we become aware of levels of consciousness we never dreamed of and a peace we'd never known on earth. To those left behind it will seem that we are gone, but our awareness of life on earth continues during this stage as our understanding grows.

The period of orientation, during which we have a foot in both worlds, varies widely depending on attitude and level of spiritual development. Individuals who experienced little or no spiritual receptivity or advancement on earth and who have little consciousness beyond their own bodies, and who died in great fear, will experience a greater time period of orientation. These earthbound souls have a far greater adjustment to make before they become willing to accept the transformation into the non-physical realm. People who die suddenly and without preparation also tend to require a longer period of orientation.

THE EXPERTS' VIEW OF NDEs

Those who have experienced Near Death, the experts tell us, are much happier for the experience. They have discovered they are immortal beings, so they live the rest of their lives fully. There is a wonderful freedom in learning that they are eternal, continuously conscious entities that move from one lifetime to the next, always growing and progressing. They have discovered that death is simply the death of the ego and the body. The mind and spirit continue after the death of the body, growing wiser and more aware with each lifetime.

John urges us not to grieve or mourn over the death of a loved one, but rather to celebrate and rejoice, because death dependably relieves all suffering and pain and transports the soul to a higher plane of love and light. Our challenge on the earth plane, where the physical body provides valuable focus, is to give that life maximum clarity and strive for unconditional love. We need to remember that death is an illusion and not to permit it to lessen the quality of life. We should look for the love that is within each soul, and seek enrichment and deepened knowledge. We're urged to try to see death as just another beginning or transition, not a termination. Make death an ally, we're told, and prepare to gently pass forth, to breathe in the light and effortlessly pass to a higher plane.

Another very different Kevin Ryerson entity, jolly Tom MacPherson, tells us death is like a roaring in your ears. Then suddenly you are passing along a tunnel of illumination. Soon you perceive yourself present among friends, and experience a level of extra awareness and enlightenment. All past realities and thoughts are then totally transformed. He says, "You then pass along another level of illumination into the presence of higher beings. Usually you can sense religious presences that were dear to you, and all things become clear. You then immediately experience an unusual pattern of time and space and sometimes have an awareness of where your next incarnation will be...quite a fascinating sensation."

"I found there really wasn't a heaven or hell," says Tom. "Leaving the physical body was not scary at all—more disorienting than scary. Is there a hell? Heavens no. Over here it's a bit of a joke. Is there such a thing as Hell? Yes, it's called England. If there had been such a place as Hell, I would have been the first to find out about it, since I was a pickpocket, hung by the British, to discourage other pickpockets."

Still another Ryerson entity, Atun-Re, tells us death is a lot like birth. It's a passing into a higher state of existence. Both birth and death can be painful or easy—depending on one's attitude, especially one's level of fear. Your level of fear determines the level of pain. No fear means no pain. We experience joy to the degree that we don't resist the experience. We can slip gently into the next world. Death throes are only birth pangs. Both death and birth bring us into new surroundings where loved ones are waiting to tend and nurture, to create a place for us surrounded by family. There is no death, only physical passing. The real lifetime never ends. No matter what happens to the physical body, the soul does not die. It remains forever with the divine.

HOW—IDEALLY—TO LET GO

Abraham, my favorite source on the other side, says, "Wake every morning of your life raring to go, excited about the coming day, determined to feel good, directing energy toward what's wanted, deliberately attracting. Give it everything you've got—until one day you realize: 'I've achieved pretty much everything I intended to do here. I've been everywhere, done everything, thought everything I wanted, interacted with everyone—basically satisfied my desires.' By now you feel that you've achieved your life purpose. You could live on indefinitely if you could keep the energy and joy flowing at that level, but life is getting a little hard. Maybe it's time to pull the plug and pass over. That night when you go to bed, decide that you've had enough of this life, decide to awake blissfully on the other side. That's all there is to it.

"Most people die because they can't stand their lives. They can't stand this, they can't stand that. But they don't die quickly or easily because they're locked into such negative vibrations. They have to suffer to exhaustion because they keep pushing against death, fighting it, denying it. They wear themselves out trying to figure out the how and when and where of their death, creating chaos and confusion, fearful and resisting. That's the hard way to go, though it's popular in your society. But it doesn't have to be hard. It can be easy.

"Don't wait around until you're miserable and helpless. The best way to go is On Purpose. Don't wait around for misery. When you're ready to go, say, 'I want to re-emerge into delightful non-physical. Why? Because I want to re-experience that pure positive energy. I want to return to that liquid love. I want to be whole, to know once again all I've ever known, to feel relief and freedom, to be pure essence of energy.' It's important to feel what you are saying. Your intent is to make your deepest vibrations match your words, to express pure wanting. That will bring you to the level that allows it to happen. When your desire for death is true and complete, you will drift into slumber and wake up in non-physical.

"Talk about what you want and why and it will all unfold perfectly, whether it's life or death. Everything that happens results from decisions. Death always requires a decision. But if you aim for everlasting glorious life, expressing it continually, up to the moment of your death, there will be no additional decision necessary. Your expression of deep desire is your decision to make the transition. That's the perfect set of circumstances—a cause and catalyst for your perfect easy passing. But be aware that even though you pass with perfection, many people will mourn and grieve—because to them death is terrible and frightening. Death of a loved one typically starts you seriously thinking about your own death. Then you start worrying, negatively preparing.

"But the ideal way to prepare is one day to wake up and say to yourself, 'I realize I have done it here in this lifetime! I am inspired and uplifted and happy with what

I've done. I have lived and breathed enough. I wonder what's next. It's time to find out.' Then simply switch off and switch worlds. That's what's happening when you see apparently happy, healthy young people, even kids, die suddenly. They realize they have done what they came for and are ready to move on. It's that easy, that wonderful. Just let go."

CONTROL YOUR CROAKING

"Your Guidance System, if you're listening to your feelings, will tell you when you're ready. When you feel fulfillment, when you've had enough, done enough—remembering that you don't have to do it all in this lifetime because you're coming back—just go lie down and re-emerge. You have absolute control over the time and circumstances of your croaking. The key is to connect with the matching energy and apply it, creating exactly what you desire. If you're disconnected you can't create. To consciously croak the way you really want, just connect to the stream. That's your job. Connect to the stream and then direct it. To make it really easy, spend your last few years living a blissful life. Aim to Feel Good all the time. That's the best preparation for control of an easy peaceful death.

"Violent deaths follow violent lives. You die when you vibrate in the place that allows it. You will die the way you live. If you live consciously and deliberately, that's the way you'll die—easily. If you live unconsciously and haphazardly and fearfully, that's the way you'll die—not easily. Trust the Laws of the Universe, they are utterly consistent.

165

They tell you that what you vibrate is what you live, so prepare yourself for an easy death by living a life of deliberate, joyful, conscious creation.

"You can practice by lying in bed before sleep, basking in the memory of a good day just past, a job well done, feeling deep satisfaction. Do the same thing at waking, deciding that all is well, looking forward with eager anticipation to the day ahead, intending joy and success of every kind. In this way you put yourself in position to experience a harmonious transition, to go the way you want. Waking from sleep is the same as waking on the day you were born—and re-emerging into non-physical. The sensations are the same. It's really no different.

"When you awake each morning you are literally re-emerging from non-physical into the physical world again. When you are ready to die, just close your eyes and fall into a deep final sleep with the clear intention of waking up in non-physical. Instead of expecting to awake in physical, focus on the non-physical aspect of sleep. Choose to be deliberate. The death experience is an agreement between your physical being and your non-physical Inner Being. Remember that resisting or worrying works against your success, so relax into your desire. Focus on the positive aspects of your death. Then, in this totally positive place, expect death. That's the formula for success in *any*thing you want, including death."

HOW TO DIE DELIBERATELY

"Simply say to yourself," Abraham continues, " 'I've

enjoyed this life. Now I seek the non-physical.' If it's what you truly want, you can release the body instantly by withdrawing from it. It's just a matter of making the decision when you're ready to go. You'll make that decision sooner or later. You can't escape making it. It's inevitable. So don't feel guilty about making it sooner instead of later!

"You can help yourself a lot by thinking of your body as just part of who you are. Don't think of the body as the whole me. That leads to a difficult—kicking and screaming—transition. Wean yourself from that wrong, mass-consciousness identity belief. Along with guilt and fear and unworthy feelings, it's what makes you cling to life beyond your time, inviting misery and suffering and magnified fear of death. Realize that the only important thing in this life is Feeling Good. Give that your full attention and highest priority in this life—if you want the easiest possible transition into that glorious room around the first dark corner.

"We love to watch the transformation of your re-emergence. It's wonderful to see because of the sweet relief you enjoy. In one fell swoop all your resistance is left behind, and the feelings of sudden freedom and elation are wonderful to behold as you re-emerge into wholeness!"

ALL DEATH IS SUICIDE

"Another way to think of death is merely as a withdrawal of focus from the physical body. All death is suicide, no matter how you do it, because all death requires a decision to go—and shows a deliberate desire to be somewhere else! But don't get hung up on the word 'suicide,' which has bad connotations for most of you. It's good to be consciously deliberate about death, instead of being forced by pain into an unconscious decision. If it's your clear, conscious intent to die, it will be a much more comfortable, joyful withdrawal than if it's merely to escape from this life. There's a big difference."

AFTER WE CROAK—THEN WHAT?

"What's waiting for you on the other side?" Abraham asks rhetorically. "That depends on the life you've led and your attitude at death. But don't worry, it's always wonderful! As soon as you joyfully accept it you can count on instant relief from all your physical and mental cares and woes. You can also count on an immediate sense of broader mental perspective. Individual comfort will vary once the physical focus is gone. The more positive your life, the easier your transition. Once you die it will be clear why there's no reason to fear death. You'll see the truth of the statement, 'Death does not exist,' because you'll still be conscious and aware of the essential you. There won't be nothingness or an empty void.

"You'll enjoy a wiser perspective. You'll see your society in a new way. You'll see how foolish you were to fear its wrath if you didn't conform. You'll see you wasted too much of your life fearing death and preparing for it, as well as seeking approval from others. Your culture taught you from childhood how you had to behave if you wanted to go to Heaven, to achieve success, to be worthy. It made you fear hellfire if you didn't conform. It took away your power. But none of that happened. Now you're in Heaven and your new perspective lets you see that what they told you was wrong and foolish. Now you see that all your power to create is in the now.

"Here's an example of a fairly typical death, from our perspective. This man had generally been quiet and gentle, but as the moment of his death approached he began to scream with terror, pleading and begging to be spared. Why? He was scared to death of death. His beliefs dictated his attitude at dying. He wasn't ready because he felt he was unworthy. And he was deathly afraid of nothingness. He believed his failures would take him to a terrible hellish unknown. But in the moment of his passing—as soon as physical focus was withdrawn—he donned broader perspective and saw that he was wrong. All his fears had been groundless.

"It took him awhile, because of his fears and lifelong negative beliefs, to accept his new surroundings and adapt to glorious non-physical. By then all strain and worry had disappeared. His awareness increased enormously and magically and wonderfully as his memory of all his past lifetimes was gradually restored. 'It (death) was no big deal, after all!' he marveled. 'If I had known it was going to be like this, I'd have come a helluva lot sooner!' Now he was experiencing the absolute ecstasy of non-physical. It can be just as glorious in the physical world if you understand and live by the Laws of the Universe—if you're truly in harmony with your desires and determined to feel good.

"Most of you, like this gentleman, are in a lackful place at the moment of your death—negatively focused in the extreme—which makes your transition a little harder at first, before you relax and begin to enjoy yourself. Most of you finally got old enough and sick enough that you couldn't continue before you finally gave up and let go. You were finally forced to make the decision to die. You had no choice.

"How much better it would be not to wait until you had no choice. Long before your life became unbearable you could have said, 'I've had all I want of this lifetime, so off I go to whatever comes next,' then enjoy an easy glorious transition...while all those you left behind are moaning and weeping and complaining. They think death is always tragic, especially if you're young and healthy. But who cares what they think. It's none of their business if you want to move on before you're suffering and ancient. Wouldn't they be amazed if they knew what you're enjoying!

"The perfect way to pass over is with an attitude of extraordinary appreciation for life, never forgetting that life is eternal. Set forth your clear intent to re-emerge back into the pure pool of non-physical energy for the purpose of someday re-emerging again. By knowing what you want and why you want it, rather than doing it from a negative place of what you don't want, you'll make the transition easier and more joyful.

"It may be interesting to note that at the moment of death, while you're still physically focused, you initially see what you expected to see—what you anticipated and expected. It may be Hell or Purgatory or the devil—or angels. Your lifelong beliefs about death and the hereafter have probably programmed you with certain strong expectations. These expectations are fulfilled—like those of any and all strong beliefs—at death, but only in the beginning. They are soon replaced by the unimaginable 'reality' of the heavenly non-physical realm, with its light and peace and freedom and love, its greatly expanded awareness and restored memory, not to mention reunions with loved ones.

"It may also be of interest that what you think of as insanity and dementia and conditions like Alzheimer's represent a process of withdrawing by people who have been overwhelmed by pain and suffering but who hang on to life out of fear and/or feeling too unworthy to depart life. They simply turn their attention away from what brings them pain and put their focus of attention on what brings them peace. Pretty smart! Their condition can last for years, living in a sort of limbo if they're too afraid of death or feel too unworthy to let go of life.

"What it's like right after you die? You feel like you're floating in an unusually vivid dream, with an utter lack of resistance. Your consciousness joyfully expands into a broader perspective. You have unlimited access to your memory of past lives, the thoughts of other people, to the wisdom of the ages, the importance of love—everything!

You have powers you never imagined on earth. Your consciousness, your personality, your perspective are all bigger than you've ever imagined.

"Thoughts seem to have a life of their own. They become thought forms that can actually think and attract in a way that can't be conveyed, because your understanding is more limited than you know. At this stage, you now direct energy instead of summoning it, attracting more of it than you ever thought possible. Your capacity for allowing it is greater than you have known, and it will grow steadily with use. Playing with energy is so fascinating that everything else seems less interesting. All you want to do is create. The only thrill now is summoning energy, deliberately flowing it and feeling uplifted."

AFTER-DEATH CHOICES

"As we keep saying," reminds Abraham, "because you don't seem to realize it, you can't kill the life force. Life runs in cycles. Death is just the end of one cycle. Nothing is more natural and inevitable than what you call death. It's more a beginning than an ending, because it's a step upward and forward, not backward or down. When you re-emerge into non-physical, you regain full participation in the Life Force—including a prodigious memory. You slip into sweet relief and strong feelings of well-being. Death restores perfect balance, so relax and accept it. Once you adjust, you're going to enjoy what it brings you!

"When you pass over you take with you all that's positive and conscious and good, leaving behind your body and all your lifetime negative habits of thought. All the positive experience of your lifetime just concluded is now added to the experience of all you've known before in your previous lives.

"Most of you do almost everything from a negative place—especially dying. You wait to re-emerge into non-physical until your body is so broken and tired that it cannot continue, or because you're in so much pain that you can't endure it, or because you're so bored with your limited physical experience that you don't want to be there anymore. Focusing on the negative—-fear, anger, unworthiness, uncertainty—gets you stuck. So you linger unhappily and in discomfort for a long time prior to re-emerging, procrastinating, putting off death until you can find a really good justification for going.

"If you are well connected to the stream of energy at your death, if your Guidance System is working and intact, if you are open and accepting and eager for new experience—then your passing will be easy and you'll rapidly expand into delicious, greater, broader knowing, where you'll find you can focus on many more things at once. The feeling experience will not be so different from physical life. You'll receive an overview of all you have been, and you'll focus on the best parts. You'll find you are multidimensional now.

"The biggest difference you'll discover in non-physical is your greater capacity and broader perspective and your freedom and relief from ailments, limitations and negativity. Non-physical is purely positive and joyous, so worry is unknown.

"Some of you worry about coming back for another lifetime. You're sure you won't want to. Don't worry about that now. Deciding now is like asking a newborn baby to choose its life purpose. You can't know what decisions you will make in non-physical. So trust that all is and will be well. You will do what you want when the time comes. When you're ready to return you'll feel an eagerness to go forth and experience from a new perspective. You'll return to make decisions, to have a glorious time on a planet that offers infinite variety. There's so much to choose from, and nothing is pre-decided. You physical beings are fearful and push against experience, while here in non-physical our eager motto is, 'Give me more!' "

YOUR LIFE'S PURPOSE

Abraham continues, "You came into this lifetime with the general intent to be joyful and uplifted, and to contribute to your culture as part of the leading edge of thought. You sought unique, personal, emphatic experiences, to uncover new desires, to add to the sum of knowledge in the universe. When you came you knew this life was a 'creating ground,' not a 'proving ground.' Its great contrast and choice make earth the best place to create. That's your general purpose. (We define creation as holding a thought, identifying the desire, then achieving vibrational harmony with that thought.) You also had a specific purpose in coming. Your Guidance System can help you find it. When you chance to cross the path of your specific intent, it always feels wonderfully right and good. You have important work here. To find it, seek out what feels good.

"We in non-physical have vibrational sensors that are ultimately much more finely developed and satisfying than mere seeing and hearing and smelling and tasting. But we also have the benefit of looking through your eyes, hearing with your ears, borrowing your other senses. But feeling is the key, in our world as well as yours. We're trying to teach you to have it all, to learn by feeling the energy through your solar plexus, like we do. Then you're following your bliss.

"Some of you may wonder why we don't dwell on your past lives. It's because that's ancient history and can't be changed. We're interested in what's happening now, because now is the only time in which you can create.

"Many of you who have begun to accept that life is eternal and death is nothing to fear, wonder how you can help a frightened, dying loved one. Here's an example. This man is old and has been sick for seven years. He keeps saying he wants to die, even asks for pills to kill him, and insists he doesn't belong here and ought to be dead, but he doesn't respond when his children urge him to 'just let go.' It's because he feels so unworthy. He feels he hasn't done enough, accomplished enough, done what he came here to do—though he has no idea what that purpose might be. Like most of you, he makes far too much of death.

" 'Death' to you is overloaded with vague meaning,

175

even more so than 'dollars' or 'sex.' Your feelings about death are so immense that when someone you know dies it gets you upset; it aggravates your precarious sense of vulnerability. You have this exaggerated sense of beginnings (birth) and endings (death) that trap you into frightening and limited beliefs. It isn't that way at all. You're just hung up on life as purely physical, with an absolute ending when the body dies. Forget that nonsense. Don't think about ending. We want you to know that you're always moving forward.

"The first step for all of you is to accept that life is everlasting, eternal, never ending. That will demolish a lot of your fears. Then accept that you're coming back, that life on earth isn't over, you'll get another chance—in fact many chances—so you don't have to feel unworthy because you think you didn't get much done in this lifetime. You accomplished more than you think. Don't judge yourself by other people's standards. All this will be clear as soon as your transition to non-physical is complete.

"So what can you do to comfort a dying father? Try to ease his fear. Paint him a pretty picture of what you believe will be coming next for him. Talk about the ecstasy and freedom of relief from all his pains and cares. Tell him you almost swoon at the thought of re-emerging into the peace and tranquility and well-being that awaits. Remind him of the coming reunion with friends and relatives. Help him feel that it's time for him to return to the joy and wisdom that's waiting. You might say something like, 'Dad, you've done all you can do in this lifetime. You've had a wonderful life, and I am grateful for the time we have shared. I'm excited at the adventure that you are beginning. I believe that you'll find it delightful beyond words. I will never forget you. Every day I will think about you on your great new journey.' By speaking these soothing words you will help release his resistance, and he will finally relax into that serene non-physical energy. Envision his easy transition. Don't feel guilty. Don't worry that by helping your father you'll be put in the same cell with Dr. Kevorkian. You're not killing him, you're just helping him make an overdue decision to let go, end his suffering and pass to a better place.

"Now let's look at a 96-year-old blind Christian grandma who has mixed feelings about death. She feels she's ready but is unsure about making the transition, thanks to a lifetime of misinformation. If only she knew that death brings the ultimate joy. A grandson wonders what he can do to help her let go. There's so much good news. If she could only know that in one fell swoop she'll be leaving behind all doubt, fear, guilt, blame, inhibition and frustration. That she's headed toward ecstatic feelings of well-being, deep knowing that all is well, and peace beyond description. Little does she know that the death experience is greatly underrated, while birth is overrated. Actually, just the reverse is true! Don't rush out and jump off the roof, but death is a lovely experience, much preferred by non-physicals over birth.

"In your society, unfortunately, death is all bad, something reserved for murderers, enemies and bad people. Your mistaken views are a reflection of your irrational fears. They cause you to make suicide illegal and death a punishment or penalty. You kill people for killing! You mourn and grieve when good people die, especially if they're young. No wonder you can't come to terms with death. But don't try to explain all that to Grandma. There's too much, and it's too difficult and too late to try to undo her lifetime of negative beliefs about death.

"But you can help Gram enormously by holding her in your attention as you imagine her triumphant transition into non-physical. If you're focused and connected to the positive stream, you're more powerful in effect than a thousand who aren't or are focused on her struggle. Envision her relief, her joy, her sense of self, her delight in her recognition that she's still here with her consciousness still intact. Imagine her refocusing into this free, clear, full, joyous place when she realizes that death has been completely misunderstood. Not only will your heart sing, you will help her with your attention to her easy peaceful passing.

"Say to her—or send a note for someone else to read—'I had a dream that released all my own fear of death. It's hard to explain, but I came to know that death is something to look forward to when the time finally comes. There's much more I want to do in this lifetime, but I find a part of me envies your coming passage, the adventure of your journey. I look forward with excitement to rediscovering all the joy that's waiting up ahead. I'm anticipating your joyful release from all your cares into something wonderful. I don't know how we became so afraid of death, of something so inevitable. Ever since my dream, this fear of death seems illogical. Now I see that it's foolish to dread death. Given the goodness of God, it seems irrational to cling to this terrible fear. I believe that God is waiting to welcome us in death. I'm excitedly anticipating that. And one day, not so long from now, I'll join you there, and we'll happily romp together again.'

"Express all this from your deep knowing, your conviction. Show her you're no longer afraid of death and you want her to know it, to feel it. Make her understand how ridiculous this fear of death has been all along. Let her hear it from your heart. It will help her relax and enjoy a more peaceful last few days and an easier transition.

"Now we have a terrified 87-year-old father who feels terribly unworthy and convinced of his failure. His son reports that he is totally without joy and fears a punishment in Hell far worse than the hell he is living here on earth. His physical inability to take action—to take care of himself—only increases his feeling of unworthiness. How can his son help him? The challenge is to raise his self-esteem by convincing him that his life has had value and importance. Say to him something like this. 'You have been a kind of model for me all my life, Dad, a guidepost whose values I have lived by.' Go back to your childhood memories and tell him how you felt. Find good things you attribute to his guidance. Make him see the seeds that he planted in you and how they have grown to nurture you. Tell him about the successes in your life that happened because of his training, because he was there for you. Connect with your Inner Being and you'll say the perfect words—and he'll feel your message.

"He'll feel validated, worthy, justified in existence. He'll let go of the anger, fear and hatred that have disconnected him from his Inner Being. You can't fill his void, but you can help him reconnect to his Inner Being by bringing back self-esteem and feelings of worthiness. Talk to him over a period of days, for just a few minutes each time. Don't overload him. Your message will take some digesting. Leave him to chew on your words and his feelings. Your dominant intent is to bring him to a place where he feels good each time you come.

"Tell him good things about non-physical—like when he gets there he'll still be able to see you and know what you're doing. Explain that when you really feel good you'll be able to connect with him, and you've been practicing because you're looking forward to connecting with him. Make it clear you'll initiate these reunions, to take all responsibility off him. Tell him he's going to re-emerge into a good place, but the better he feels at the moment of death the easier, more pleasant and joyful his transition will be. So it makes good sense to keep trying to Feel Good.

"To bolster his feelings of worthiness, say 'We've all done the best we could every step along the way.' You'll get so you recognize when he's connected to the stream and his Inner Being. He'll be visibly up. In one of those good moments say, 'See, Dad, how good you feel right now? I believe that's what death is like—Feeling Good. You know that fear feels bad, but I don't believe there's anything to be afraid of. The place you're going is good, and when you get there you're going to enjoy complete relief from everything that's bothering you now.' And don't forget to remind him that the better he feels, the better and easier and more peaceful his passage.

"You can explain that worthiness has different definitions, public and private. We were asked why a man with a public reputation as a noble, church-going, do-gooder suffered such an agonizing death. We explained that the picture of him drawn by society was distorted. Society was misled, so the newspapers told you what a great man he was, publicly. But privately he was something very different. He died violently because that's the way he privately lived. Privately is what counts, so don't waste your time currying favor and seeking approval to create a shiny public image.

"Near-Death-Experiences are always 'creation by default' that happen to disconnected people living dangerously but not yet ready to die. The experience shocks them into a profound reassessment of their lives. It's a shocking confrontation between their Inner Being and their physical body. NDEs can happen during surgery or even sleep. A new zest for life often results from making the decision

PEACEFUL PASSING

to remain in physical, allowing a potent new energy connection. The person somehow realizes that there's far greater contrast on earth than in non-physical. Nothing in the Universe is better for creating than the bliss of consciousness in the physical realm, and nothing is worse than the total disconnection when life has no purpose.

"The goal of 'ascension' is popular with people who think they can take their bodies with them so they won't have to come back for future lifetimes. They're worried about having to start over at the beginning. They just can't conceive that their beliefs and intentions will be different (far wiser and broader) once they're in non-physical. The belief in ascension comes from a place of lack. You can't take your body with you. Ascension involves lowering your resistance while raising your vibrations to reduce the difference between physical and non-physical—in order to enjoy an easier passage. And that much is good and true. But it makes far too much of both death and birth. Life is for living, not preparing for death. They would be better advised to spend their lives happily exploring and having fun.

"To them—and to all of you—we say Just Feel Good and stay connected—and you can't possibly go wrong. Life will be joyful and easy! We promise."

There you have it—sage advice and specific instruction on how (and why) to take full control of your perfect, peaceful passing, free of fear and full of joyful anticipation—from the only real authorities on death and non-physical. You've heard their siren song of the afterlife, the blandishments and incentives of the hereafter—sweet unimaginable relief, genuine peace, freedom of every kind, restored prodigious memory back through the ages, wisdom, new closeness to the fount of all creation, greatly enhanced awareness and consciousness—even bliss and enlightenment. It's all waiting to welcome you when you cross over from this lifetime into delightful non-physical.

In Chapter 9, I'll help you digest and consider experimenting with the many new ideas you've been exposed to—the revolutionary concepts and the exciting possibilities they open up. To help you figure out how to apply what you've learned, I'll tell you how I've integrated these teachings from the other side to broaden and sweeten my own life. Then, in Chapter 10, I'll offer my credentials for writing this book, give you a taste of the success I've enjoyed, and talk about my personal intentions for Letting Go peacefully and easily when the time is right for me.

~

"Death is slumber."

–SHELLEY

"Life well used brings Happy death."

–LEONARDO DE VINCI

9

SUMMARY, REVIEW & APPLICATION

We've heard from the experts that we can take control of death, and that the afterlife is heavenly, not hellish. But how do we use this astounding information? Where do we start? The way to begin, says Abraham, is to make friends with death. Turn your former enemy into an ally. Since death is inescapable, why not relax and prepare to enjoy it? That's what I did.

So why not start now to pave the way for an easy, peaceful passing by changing your beliefs about old devil death? By changing your attitude you can demolish all your death-related fears. That's the first step on the road toward an easy happy passing, toward the goal of taking back control over death and making a smooth trauma-free crossing into the delightful hereafter.

There are plenty of good reasons for shaking hands and making up with death. If you accept the testimony—as I do—of the only true authorities on the subject, you see that death can be something to look forward to when the time is right, not something to dread. Here's a digest of the message contained in Chapters 7 and 8.

If we define death as "the end," then there isn't any death. It doesn't exist because only the body dies. Life is everlasting, eternal, never ending. Death is just the end of a cycle, the shifting from the earthly plane to a higher one, a transformation from physical to non-physical.

Though the body dies, it's just part of who we are. The mind and spirit and eternal consciousness live on. Death is just birth into a higher state of existence. It's more beginning than ending, a step up to perfect balance where any sense of unworthiness vanishes. Because life never ends, there's no need to feel unworthy about a lack of achievement. You go around more than once, so you don't have to sweat imagined failures in this lifetime. There are plenty more chances to get it right up ahead. Death is actually easier than birth, say the experts. It's the ultimate joy, because in one fell swoop you get across-the-board, unimaginable relief, leaving behind all doubt, fear, guilt, blame, inhibition and frustration—not to mention complete freedom from suffering and illness. What could top that?

Probably only life in the hereafter! After all that freedom and relief comes a great new marvelous adventure—a loving, light-filled welcome where all failures are forgiven and personal forgiveness becomes effortless. With the growing awareness that there's no punishment or hell, no matter the depth of your earthly sins, there comes the restoration of forgotten wisdom, the return of your prodigious memory of past lifetimes, fantastic new powers, reunions with loved ones, nurturing bliss, a broader mental perspective... and more.

There's enrichment beyond belief, entrance into a glorious higher awareness and consciousness, the discovery that all fears are groundless. By now you're a multidimensional being, with powers you never dreamed of on earth, in a place sweeter and more abundantly loving than any heaven you've ever heard of, where worry is unknown and negativity is a thing of the past.

To me, the heavenly new life that awaits us all is more than ample reason to stop dreading death and the hereafter. Once we slip easily into the afterlife, the shackles of fear fall away, the brakes on life get released, and we're fully free to live the rest of our lives feeling more alive than ever before. So why not kiss and make up with death?

CASHING IN: PRACTICAL APPLICATIONS

What's the next step? For me, it's testing and learning more about the New Way of Creating, adopting and integrating the teachings to find fun and success in the rest of your life. Before it's time to "cash in" for your easy, peaceful passing, it makes sense to "cash in" on the incredible benefits available from the New Way Of Creating that the experts have taught us—benefits beyond belief! After all, our traditional action-based belief system—with its loopholes for luck and fate—has proved to be less than effective at creating happiness and success. Actions, it turns out *don't* speak louder than words!

So why not deliberately create what you want instead of settling for random results? Good feelings create success of every kind. Feeling Good is the shortcut because it's both the means and the end. Dwell on tragedy, disaster, failure and fear and you'll eventually attract it. The potential for deliberate creating is absolutely unlimited, well beyond imagining for most of us. Abraham assures us that we can quite literally be or have or do *any*thing we want! *Anything!*

Miracles beyond miracles are truly within reach. For instance, we can reverse illness and aging to achieve youthfulness and perfect health. Weight loss and fitness can be realized without diet or exercise. Real success in relationships and career are now readily achievable. Happiness, fun, wealth, playfulness, leisure, safety and freedom—you name it—can all be created by employing the New Way. Theoretically, you can even live forever. You don't have to die if you can overcome aging, disease and the overpowering mass-consciousness belief that death is unavoidable. I know you can control the weather because I do it all the time! It's just a matter of beliefs. There aren't any limits to what can be created.

That's just a taste of the breathtaking, stunning possibilities opened up by putting the New Way of Creating to work. We'll look at most of these possibilities in more detail down the road when we examine what I've personally been able to achieve.

The only limitations on what can be created are those we impose on ourselves—the limitations on what we can expect, the negative focus of our attention, and the limitations imposed by our lifetime negative beliefs...plus the timid mediocrity of our desires.

But deep, clear, passionate desire can be reawakened. Limiting beliefs can be changed, discreated and replaced. And positive expectation can be stretched and developed. All it takes is desire for a happier life and the determination to grab this opportunity to reach for it. The tools are ready and waiting for anybody. *Any*body! There are no prerequisites beyond desire. You don't have to be smart or adult or educated, and it's never too early or too late to begin.

How do you begin? I suggest you Review Chapter 5, THE WAY THINGS WORK, and Chapter 6, WE CREATE OUR REALITY, with a new purpose. The first time around they were just foundation and framework for finding out how to take control of your death. Now that you know how to do that, why not try reading them to improve the quality of your life, the success and the good feelings you'd like to enjoy for the rest of your days? Remember that any progress you make will also pave the way for the easiest possible death.

It's a win-win, double-benefit, can't lose situation. It's even fun and exciting! Abraham insists that the exploration and contemplation of principles and beliefs is man's greatest source of joy. I've found that to be true.

Instead of rehashing Chapters 5 and 6, I'm going to tell you about how I've applied their teachings, and the enormous benefits they've brought me. Those benefits are my credentials for writing this book. If you read the Introduction, you'll know I found my way to the concept of controlled Letting Go by projecting the belief system condensed in Chapters 5 and 6. You can benefit from my experience by using this foundation and framework to build a solid basis for (1) success in the rest of your life and (2) an easy controlled death and (3) making a smooth adjustment to life in the hereafter.

TEST THE NEW WAY

You needn't accept the contents of those two chapters on faith. You can test them in two ways. Test One: Consult your Guidance System. Your wise loving Inner Being (i.e., the essential you, your soul or spirit) will always direct you to your best course of action for reaching your goals. It speaks through your feelings and emotions. It's foolproof guidance, but it doesn't shout. If you're not always aware of your feelings—and none of us are—you'll have to listen hard. You'll have to make an effort to be sensitive to how you feel. Then simply do what feels good and avoid what feels bad, as explained in more detail in Chapters 5 and 6.

Listen to your heart and your feelings—not to "shoulds," "ought to's" and "duty" as defined by others. In addition to fear, seeking the approval of others is the biggest obstacle to happiness and success. Do what makes *you* Feel Good. Period! If the teachings and explanations you've heard here feel right, your Inner Being is giving them its seal of approval. Trust and follow your Guidance System's direction in everything you do. Your Inner Being is your wisest, finest most dependable you. It has only your best interests at heart, continuously seeking your happiness and personal growth. It will offer you guidance on every decision. That's how you test validity and rightness. There isn't any risk. Just follow your feelings. Because they represent your deepest desires, you can safely trust and act on them.

Test Two: Experiment with the teachings. Try them out to see if they work. "The proof is in the pudding." Unlike our physical authorities on life and death, they have no hidden agendas. Remember that test of the Law of Attraction toward the end of Chapter 6? You were invited to try to create a parking space in a crowded parking lot, attracting it in advance so it would be waiting when you arrive. Why not go back and try it? Or create something similar that might be more appropriate to your situation.

The key to success is generating positive expectation that the space will be waiting. So don't overreach by asking for the moon . Choose to create something reasonable, a small stretch of your beliefs, something highly possible, something you can believe in. Start small and expect to have fun. When you enjoy success, celebrate and take credit for your creation. When you succeed, you'll be excited by your newfound power. You'll have proved that expectation really does create.

YOU DIE AS YOU LIVED

In addition to creating what you want, there's another good reason for making friends with death and putting the New Way to work. The experts keep telling us, "We die the way we lived," and "Violent lives mean violent death." They say the only hell is on our side of the fence, and the afterlife is dependably wonderful—once you make the adjustment. But that adjustment, we're told, can be difficult and protracted if you go to your death kicking and screaming, petrified that it's the end with nothing but nothingness yawning ahead, or some kind of endless hell or purgatory waiting to punish you for a lifetime of sins. If life, to you, is inextricable from the body and you're convinced that "We only go around once," then clearly death will *not* be easy and peaceful. Be warned!

So a little preparation for death is advisable, especially because it's guaranteed to make the rest of your life happier and more successful. I'm not talking about the arduous lifelong preparation of Hindus and Buddhists who hope to generate good karma and gain the status of enlightenment, thus escaping the need to return for more unwanted lifetimes. Or the similarly motivated endeavors of would-be Ascensionists. I'm talking about striving to Feel

Good more of the time and to live in greater harmony with the Laws of the Universe as set forth by the channeled entities quoted in this book.

Why? Because spiritual growth in this lifetime and the greater happiness and success that it generates seem to make the difference between an easy, peaceful passing and a slow, miserable, fearful death when you can't hang on any longer. And as we saw in Chapter 8, there's a big difference in both the welcome you get and the initial phase of life in the hereafter.

But whatever your preparation—from lifelong devotion to a total lack of effort—you can count on sweet relief from all your earthly cares and afflictions, a warm loving welcome, total forgiveness, an absence of negativity and judgment, the return of your vast memory, effortless access to universal wisdom...and all the other perks mentioned earlier. In Chapter 10 we'll take a look at the not unimpressive success I've enjoyed in every area of my life as a direct result of practicing the New Way/U-View. That success constitutes my credentials for writing this book.

$\sim$

"Death where is thy sting?"

–CORINTHIANS: BIBLE

"Die all, die merrily."

–SHAKESPEARE

10

MY CREDENTIALS, MY LIFE AND MY DEATH

Y ou might wonder about my credentials for writing this book. I don't have a Masters in Death or a Ph.D. in Channeled Entities, but you can blame that on the narrowness of academia. I'm just a professional writer of 46 years whose first nine books have sold more than a quarter-million copies. Of course, the really important data in this book—the meat—isn't mine. It comes from the other side. I just came up with the idea of an upbeat book on death from the viewpoint of the only real authorities on the subject.

I had discovered that those who pass for authorities in our culture don't seem to know what they're talking about. And they do us a huge disservice when they insist on wrapping death in grief, fear, shame and guilt—often for their own ends. The resulting disastrously negative beliefs rob us of the joy of life, scaring us into living our lives with the brakes on. They intimidate us into premature aging and terminal illness just to dutifully earn an honorable excuse for dying. They're responsible for untold misery and suffering. I'd like to counter some of that. That's why I wrote this book.

There's no way to check credentials of the entities who speak to us from the beyond, but you can easily test their message as discussed above. They are trying to help us by sharing their vastly greater wisdom and experience—because they love us and therefore want to ease our suffering. They have given us two perfectly splendid ways to test their assertions. That's all they can do. We can take it or leave it. My credentials are a slightly different matter. The same two tests also apply to what I say. If it feels good and works for you, that's all the validation that's possible. Trust your feelings.

But maybe I can supply some assurance that they work by telling you something of my life—and the modest success I attribute to using the New Way to create what I want and to avoid major setbacks. After I discovered the New Way about 15 years ago, I gradually switched over from fun-less, hard-driving physical action (work) to vastly easier mental-emotional creating and Feeling Good. To show you my success in various aspects of life—which I attribute to the teachings—I'm going to have to brag quite a bit. But don't hang up on that. Look for the connection between my efforts to create and the success created.

WHO IS THIS GUY, WOOD?

I've always been an independent, ask-questions kind of guy who wasn't afraid to go his own way. When I didn't like the rules because they seemed unfair or made me feel bad, I often rebelled, without regard for the consequences. I didn't feel I had any choice. Doing what felt right was more important than gaining approval. My freedom from the approval trap and a relative lack of fear clearly helped me create. I'm less afflicted than most by caring what other people think. As Abraham explains, dependency on outside validation—reliance on the good opinion of others—instead of building it inside, is a major obstacle to the development of freedom, joy and growth.

For instance, when I was still a teenager I was nagged by my mother into taking an indoctrination class for joining her church, but I asked so many pointed questions—and argued so much with the preacher about his answers—that I was politely asked not to come back.

In college I innocently joined a fraternity, but my discovery of institutionalized cruelty and dishonesty caused me to lead a pledge class revolt before I resigned. Majoring in forestry because of my love of the woods and mountains, I stubbornly studied only what appealed to me without regard for my professors' assignments or exams. As a result, I graduated with the lowest grade point average in the history of the school. Then I took a tramp steamer to Europe with money I'd saved working the summer before in a construction camp in the Alaskan arctic. After traveling on the continent all summer with two aspiring writers, I returned determined to become a writer myself—though I had prided myself a few months earlier on getting through the university without taking a single course in hated English!

In those days I didn't know I'd "accidentally" stumbled (society's explanation) into the essentials for successful creating. I now believe I was following directions from my Inner Being, being nudged toward intentions I'd held coming into this lifetime. I was willing to act on my strong desires, to rely on inner direction rather than outer. I was utterly convinced I must follow my own path, no matter what. And I halfway expected success. So my *modus operandi* wasn't far from Abraham's formula for creating.

That has to explain why I managed—against staggering odds—to attract a job as a magazine editor in San Francisco at age 22. I found it fun and easy, but I quit two years later to hitchhike to Mexico City to write sensitive (but bad) short stories and my first (unpublished) book. After I came back, I worked my way by age 30 to Staff Correspondent for *Time, Life* and *Sports Illustrated.*

That same year I got married and made my first real estate investment, a rundown fixer-upper duplex. I did so well in investment real estate that I was able to retire five years later at the age of 34 from Time, Inc.; buying myself still more independence. Now I only worked for myself and my family, but I helped a number of my friends use the same investment strategy to escape the rat race into early retirement. A few years later I started writing books.

My first five books were about the outdoors—a wilderness trail guide and two bestseller backpacking books. By then I had a cabin in the High Sierra, accessible only by boat or trail, on the edge of the wilderness, where I spent the summer quarter of the year with my daughter, writing and playing in the country I loved. Later, I wrote books about my passage through Primal Therapy and my discovery of the powerful but gentle medical system called homeopathy.

In my fifties I decided to become a whitewater river guide, wrote a book about the adventure and married a young lady who loved the outdoors and saw no obstacle in the 20 year difference in our ages. By now my money was invested in low management apartment complexes and malls, so I was totally free to play and travel with my new playmate.

All my life I'd been searching without success for a belief system I could accept without reservation. I'd investigated and tried out most of the world's major religions and was almost resigned to settling for Agnostic Pantheism, when I stumbled on the channeled entity Lazaris fifteen years ago. His message: "We each create our entire reality and we do it with thought, not action," rung my bell, resonating perfectly with my feelings.

To my amazed delight, this new belief system fit like the proverbial glove. It felt like going home to something I'd always known but had somehow forgotten. For the next eight years I endeavored to integrate this new and exciting belief system into my life.

Then a friend gave me an introductory tape to the channeled entity Abraham. Here was a vastly clearer, warmer, more detailed, more appealing presentation of the same philosophy—an even better fit. Stimulated and excited, I met and got acquainted with Abraham's channel, Esther Hicks. When she launched a periodical called *The Leading Edge (TLE)* I was permitted to write the only column from this side, appropriately titled "Human Perspectives."

When I turned 60, I got a major chance to test my new beliefs. Like many in our culture, I had decided that my sixtieth birthday ushered in old age. I had led an extremely active life to that point, but maybe it was time to slow down. I couldn't expect to keep up the pace, which included competitive basketball as well as mountain climbing and tennis. It was time to kick back and gracefully accept life's inevitable limitations, to find more sedentary and passive pursuits. I tried that for about a month, but I felt irritable and restless...until I decoded the message.

My Guidance System was telling me unmistakably that I wasn't yet ready to start the slow slide toward death. Not even close! My GS was giving me just the opposite message. I wanted greater capability, not less. I wanted youth! It was a wake-up call I won't soon forget. Happily, I had the tools and the beliefs to reverse my field and create what I wanted. As soon as I resolved to grow younger, not older, I felt great again.

GROWING YOUNGER

On paper I experimented with putting my deepest feelings and ardent desires into words. When I'd developed a paragraph that both embodied my intent and stimulated my feelings of youth and radiant health, I put this affirmation to work for me—willing my desire into genuine expectation. I knew that merely mouthing words wouldn't bring success. As I wrote in Abraham's *The Leading Edge*, "Mere repetition and recitation don't work. (That's why prayer has such a poor track record.) The Universe knows—from my thoughts—what I want. I find it helpful to remember that the Universe doesn't speak English or do numbers. And I can't generate joy and explain at the same time."

It's absolutely essential to match words with strong feelings. The Universe responds to vibration and emotion, attention and expectation, not words. I don't deliver my affirmations unless I'm brimming with good feeling and able to match my words with emotion. Energetically acting out the words generates the essential emotional content. I literally dance my affirmations.

As I wrote in *TLE*, "I vigorously nod, grin, jump up and down and shout Yes! with all my heart. Feeling Good, after all, is the bottom line—both the end and the means of success. And I strive to make negativity trigger my awareness like a jolt of electricity, a bucketful of cold water—alert for the warnings that bad feelings bring. It's much easier, I've found, to dodge negativity than it is to create such slippery and elusive concepts as freedom, love, joy and growth."

What's the result of this program? Now, at 70, I feel younger, more youthful, more vibrantly alive, more capable and energetic, than I did at 60. I know the cells in my body listen and obey my desire and emotion. The message they received was to reverse the aging process, and they have. I do everything I did ten years ago—except play high contact basketball with kids—and much more. I have literally rolled back the clock by determinedly creating youth, by rejecting the gloomy mass consciousness, self-fulfilling belief in inevitable aging. I play a couple of sets of singles tennis every day or two with my wife, and we walk or hike every day in the relatively high altitude of our two homes.

And I'm not straining. I don't get as tired as I used to because, knowing that I can be or have or do anything I want, I know I don't have to tire. Getting tired comes from the overpowering (but never questioned) expectation and belief of mass consciousness that you must tire from exercise—and tire quicker when you're older. Not so. I simply invoke my expectation of tirelessness, immunity from fatigue and easy flowing freedom. I know that the unquestioned necessity of "training for fitness" is just one more sad belief. I used to do all kinds of boring, arduous exercises and running to get myself "in shape." Not any more. I've dumped that limiting belief. Now I'm fit for anything I want to do—by simply expecting to be fit. Unlikely as that may sound, I've proved that it works. I only wish I'd started at age 40 instead of 60. Age 20 would have been even better.

FORGET DIET!

The same goes for diet. Dieting is for people who fear fat, and it's one of the most pernicious, disastrous, misery-making beliefs to be found in our culture. I eat exactly what I want, when I want, with no limitations. And I stay both fit and slim. My body in silhouette—to hide the thinning hair and gray beard—could pass for that of a 35-year-old athlete. I stand 5'11"—a full inch taller than I stood ten years ago!—and weigh 155 pounds. I stand tall and straight, vigorous and proud. Yet I ignore diet and training and cholesterol and all the myriad fears that surround food, fat and eating. For instance, last year I enjoyed a Chocolate Sundae every night of the week. Now I customarily have a milkshake every day with my lunch. I also eat a ton of butter, but I'm safe from excess cholesterol and fat because I haven't the slightest fear of them. I don't put on weight because I don't expect to.

How can I do this? It's simple. My beliefs and expectations about food make it easy. I genuinely believe that my body will dependably extract all the energy I need from whatever I choose to eat and assimilate it perfectly, letting all the unwanted bulk and weight pass through and away. And it does. That's the only belief needed. I have the abundant energy I desire, and my weight remains the same no matter what I eat. I need no regular vitamins, minerals or supplements, and I don't share the culture's destructive fear of foods that "they say" are "bad for you."

My New Way belief supplies a marvelous freedom from

a lifetime of restrictive beliefs about food and drink. Most of us are cursed with individual, often negative beliefs about hundreds, maybe thousands, of food substances. Think about it. Name a few foods and note your strong beliefs about each. Get the picture? The New Way lets you escape from all those limiting beliefs, restoring the freedom to eat for pleasure and perfect health.

SEEKING PERFECT HEALTH

When you're sick or old or in some way afflicted, there's nothing you yearn for like relief from your symptoms. Of course, death brings that relief, but if you're not yet ready to depart, the New Way offers just as great a potential. But it isn't easy. Creatively curing ailments is difficult because it's hard for us humans to remove our attention and expectation from constant chronic symptoms. When your back hurts all the time it's nearly impossible not to notice it. So an ounce of prevention is worth a ton of cure.

Because its hard to heal pain, it's vastly preferable to invest in that ounce of prevention, which comes from regularly summoning and expecting Perfect Health. I try to remember to dance my perfect health affirmation often when I'm feeling really good, because I've learned the hard way how difficult it can be to get rid of nagging symptoms. That's when it's easiest and works best.

Merely "intending perfect health" seems insufficient to most people. We're so used to attacking what we don't want—shouting "No!" even though it's counter-productive—that we're inclined to do the same with our symptoms. Unfortunately, the attention (and emotion) of saying we hate them and don't want them only reinforces them! Or we employ "more is better" and overdo our demands for perfect health, unintentionally creating lack and resistance. A balance must be struck. When I get unwanted symptoms I first try to divert my attention from them, employing positive denial and optimistically minimizing the ailment's importance. I back this up with appropriate affirmations, eagerly danced when I'm symptom-free.

Incidentally, the words I use in my affirmation dance don't matter in the least. Their only purpose is to trigger my passion. The Universe knows my desires and intents very well and needs no reminding. Reminders can be dangerous because of the negative component of lack always present in desire. The Universe relies on the vibration of feelings, not words. The words I use are chosen for their ability to inspire, conjure and convey the exact feelings and meanings that match my intent and desire. Those feelings, plus desire, are what create.

DRUGS AND DOCTORS

What about drugs and doctors? For the last dozen years my wife Deanne and I have relied on the potent but safe and effective medicines of homeopathy to help keep us healthy. After a single $6 dose of a homeopathic remedy cured my devastating pollen allergy ten years ago, Deanne became a lay homeopath and I wrote an excellent introductory book on the subject (*Homeopathy: Medicine that Works!*).

If Deanne can't solve our minor problems with her arsenal of medicines, we fall back on telephone consultations with our world-renowned homeopathic M.D., Roger. So our attack on unwanted symptoms is four-pronged: (1) Optimistic minimizing and positive denial, (2) Withdrawing attention, (3) My Perfect Health and healing affirmation dances and (4) expertly prescribed homeopathic remedies. Aside from Roger, we don't have a doctor, and we never "go in for checkups" of any kind. We have a great summertime dentist, but we no longer get cleaning/checkups. I used to "need" a lot of dental work: fillings, root canals, crowns, quarterly cleaning and checkups. Not any more. In the last year our dentist has collected exactly $15! My dental care nowadays consists of expecting "tuff, strong, healthy choppers"—and not worrying.

We carry no medical insurance, having canceled it many years ago. As Abraham put it "Because good health comes from a lack of resistance and negativity, and the basis of all insurance is purely negative fear, why increase your negativity by carrying insurance?" I rely on myself to stay healthy and safe, not on insurance to pay for health care after I'm sick or injured. A belief in the need for insurance inescapably involves the fearful negative expectation of injury or illness.

DON'T GET CHECKUPS!

Abe also says "Never go to a doctor for a checkup. There's nothing more dangerous to your health! Why go to a doctor if you're not sick? Why hire an expert in detecting disease to find something wrong with you? A doctor will soon give you something to worry about. If you weren't sick beforehand, you soon will be!" Doctors and dentists are definitely dangerous to your health. We humans are terribly vulnerable to their pronouncements because we're so susceptible to suggestion. (When a new disease is described in the media, 10,000 people discover they have it the next day!) Doctors and dentists are dangerous because they're such powerful authority figures. When they diagnose trouble, it's hard to deny it attention and expectation. So you start worrying. When you worry, you're fueling the illness idea with emotion (fear) and more attention and expectation. You're soon effectively creating the condition diagnosed! Keep it up and you'll begin to experience symptoms. It's the Law of Attraction in action—the kind of attraction you don't want!

To summarize: Doctors and dentists are good at finding problems you never dreamed of—and they're eager to treat them. Their authoritative diagnosis is likely to frighten you, their prescriptions for cure are usually pessimistic—and their drugs are truly something to fear. Applying the Laws of the Universe, it becomes clear why all this produces the attention and expectations that negatively create. Why are doctors so defensively negative? First of all, they fear malpractice suits, so they try to protect themselves by holding down your expectations of cure. Secondly, they know that the expensive drugs they're pushing for the pharmaceutical companies (that fund our medical schools) are mostly ineffective. Healing and curing by today's drugs is rare. Thirdly, they know that the side effects of their drugs can be disastrous.

The term "modern medical science" would be laughable if the results weren't so tragic. Most doctors are only good mechanics, and statistics suggest that they're often unsuccessful human beings. So it's not surprising that their gloomy diagnosis, dangerous prescriptions and pessimistic warnings are more likely to harm than help. Most people would be far better off if they weaned themselves away from doctors and took greater responsibility for their own health. The New Way of creating offers unparalleled opportunity for doing just that—creating perfect health and perfect everything else.

Abraham helps with three comforting assurances: (1) Perfect health is both natural and normal for all human beings. That's the intention of the Universe in beaming pure positive energy our way. Our ailments and afflictions are aberrations produced by (i.e., attracted by) our negativity and resistance, which has interrupted or cut off the positive energy flow. (2) We have a 17-second grace period for feeling unwanted anger, fear, etc., and safely switching back to Feeling Good before negativity can begin manifesting. (3) No physical ailment or condition—no matter how chronic, advanced or seemingly permanent or threatening—is irreversible. With strong enough purely positive creating, the potential remains for restoring perfect health!

I don't claim my health is perfect, but at the moment I

haven't a single unwanted symptom. Younger people often envy my energy, fitness and activity. With that four-pronged attack I've cured innumerable ailments, including some longstanding chronic conditions, some of them within the past six months. I'm taller, straighter and stronger than I was five years ago. And the weak reading glasses I buy off the rack for poor light conditions require lower magnification each time I buy them. Twenty years ago I needed 2.75. Now I'm down to 1.25—or less.

My next book will expand on all this, addressing healing yourself and reversing aging and bodily afflictions (like fat and disease) by employing the New Way (not doctors), to help you create fitness and Perfect Health. I tentatively call it *Get Well on your Own!* (copyrighted title).

$ MONEY AND WEALTH

The measure of success in our culture, unfortunately, is still the acquisition of wealth, because money brings visible evidence of success. I've always been good at attracting money, because I like and enjoy it. Although I didn't have a lot when I was young, apparently I didn't erect the barriers of lack and negative expectancy that block most people from attracting it. As Abraham puts it, "Desire, by definition, always contains a component of lack. So continuous hungry yearning for money you don't have can easily block its acquisition." I've never earned more than $5/hour and didn't inherit until recently, but though I haven't held a job for the past 34 years my net worth runs to seven figures and my annual income to six.

Five years ago I made a concerted effort to attract money to buy an expensive house I wanted. As I wrote in my Human Perspectives column in *TLE*, "My main affirmation was (and still is), I'll have money enough to have and do *every*thing I want." I made my deadline with thousands to spare, but the money kept on coming. It got to be funny. The variety of sources showed the Universe's ingenuity in attracting money for me. I twice "found" more than $1000 in my bank account. I sold all the real estate I put on the market—fast at top prices in dead markets—for cash. Last summer, $35,000 dropped in my lap when an investment property unexpectedly refinanced. I also got a surprise tax refund, a big rebate, a court ordered refund, a surplus distribution, even an inheritance. A New York TV producer paid to dramatize one of my books, and its sales took off. And recently my wife, Deanne, won us a sweepstakes luxury trip.

RELATIONSHIPS

Money and health may be more important to older citizens, but love and relationships seem more critical to the young. I used desire and expectancy, after my divorce, to attract my lovely young wife, Deanne. I wanted a natural, unsophisticated, charming, intelligent, pretty, educated, optimistic, frank, unpretentious, vigorous, strong, healthy, outdoorsy, curious, sexy, athletic younger woman to play and travel with me—and that's what I got.

I hadn't expected a lady 20 years younger who grew up on a farm and taught home economics, but that background produced many of the qualities I wanted. She's also an enthusiastic gardener, hard-working devoted wife and mother, great cook and eager traveler. I met her on a whitewater rafting trip in 1982, and we've been together ever since. I'm still appreciating my good fortune...uh...I mean my success in attracting her into my life. Abraham endorses the saying, "To thine own self be true," urging us to be more selfish, hedonistic and narcissistic—to counter our great susceptibility to guilt and shame and the low self esteem that lets us live in fear and look for approval from others, rather than listening to our wise inner selves.

Deanne and I use Abraham's New Way teachings to deal with the inevitable stress of spending most of our time together. When one of us falls into negativity, the other is quick to supply reminders of what's wanted. We spend more time together than most couples because we enjoy each other's company and our aims are so similar. Our life together largely runs smoothly because we're both optimistically expressing our desires and expecting their manifestation. And we help and support each other. We doubly attract the positive adventure and joyful success that we intend—and we avoid the major setbacks that come with random creating. During the summer-third of the year we live in a 550-square-foot mountain cabin that produces more inescapable togetherness than most couples could tolerate. At the same time, we're highly independent and very different individuals.

We've recently used the New Way of creating to increasingly attract stimulating, remarkable, delightful, extraordinary and helpful friends into our lives. I also deliberately attract dependable, competent, professional people who can help me in my various enterprises and endeavors. For instance, when I purchased our home in Sedona (where I knew no one) I needed an all-around honest, congenial, creative, widely talented contractor to undertake the radical extensive remodeling I intended. The man I attracted was all that and more. Cliff not only contributed mightily, he supplied dependable subcontractors whose schedules fit together perfectly. We completed a beautiful job in six months that would normally have taken two years, for a third of the expected price.

When I have need of a particular commodity or service I attract it by letting my need and desire crystalize into a strong feeling clarity that will speak to the Universe.

My family relationships may also be revealing. Before returning for this lifetime I picked appropriate parents that would help me fulfill my intentions here. My father, a hard-driving, smart, football-playing, travel-loving gardener and college newspaper editor is, at this writing, a mellow 95-year old who sits smiling in his beautiful garden. In many ways I'm writing this book for him, and I've repeatedly assured him that it's okay to let go and pass over anytime—but he isn't ready yet!

My loving artist mother lavished a lot of nourishment and affection on her sickly, allergic, shy and introverted son. She was musical and determined to provide me with instruction. Though I didn't take to the piano or flute, I was successful as a singer and my happiest hours were (and are) spent singing. The zenith of my short singing career was a world premiere solo with the San Francisco Symphony in the opera house that my grandfather built. When in my forties, between books, I got a sudden urge to paint, mom provided the instruction that led to three one-man shows and the sale of more than half of my work.

When infection threatened my mother at age 88 in Berkeley, I called her frequently from Sedona, recalling the happy times we had shared, thanking her for all she'd done for me, urging her to let go of her religion-based fears and slip easily into the sweet relief of death. When her time was near and she no longer recognized people, my sister urged me to come to her deathbed. I declined. There was nothing more I could do for her, and I didn't want to see her as she was then. I only wanted to remember the good times. When she passed into non-physical, I never felt the slightest need to grieve or mourn. Instead, I rejoiced in her relief from pain and the knowledge that she was happy in the hereafter. Nowadays when I look at her paintings hanging on our walls, I happily recall the fun we had together. I often talk to her and appreciate what she did to ease and brighten and widen my life.

SAFETY VS. PROTECTION

Let me return to the matter of safety. I carry no health insurance because all insurance, as Abraham explained, is predicated on fear. Insurance salesmen claim to be selling "protection," but the need for protection is inherently based on the fear of calamities that seem beyond our control. Not true. Because I create the entirety of my reality, I believe that no one else can threaten me. I'm safe, free and in control. So I carry only the minimal home and auto insurance that is required by lenders or the law.

Speaking of the law, Abraham explains that rules and laws are just as fear-based as insurance. They're contrived by frightened people in authority who fear various possibilities. So they seek to protect themselves by making the actions they fear illegal. Negative, punitive rules and regulations are just more evidence of fear and ignorance. In our society, living in fear is considered the natural state of affairs, so protection appears to be a necessity. Sad, and untrue. The vaunted, unquestioned "Rule of Law" is in reality a rule of fear!

Man was meant to be free, Abraham tells us, to create what's wanted and needed. Laws are unnecessary if creation is understood.

Ironically, all those billions of (mostly government) signs that start with "no" are actually negatively attracting exactly what's not wanted! Though well-meaning, the various War Against Drugs, Aids, etc., are disastrously attracting the very things they want to destroy by focusing additional attention on what's not wanted. All campaigns to eradicate something feared do the same. No wonder there's so much crime, disease, confusion—and ultimately fear—in our society!

I protect myself through my focus of attention, deliberate attraction and expectation, not by caving into fear and buying insurance or relying on protection by the law. Though my holdings and ventures are extensive, complex and wide-ranging, I don't have a lawyer or any need for one. I don't attract danger, so I'm safe. You can be, too.

WORK AND CAREER

For 46 years I've been a professional writer, and I love it. *Do What You Love and The Money Will Follow*, is a title I endorse and a philosophy I've followed. It avoids all the downside of work. We're good at what we love doing. If you're wondering what to do with your life or are sick of what you're doing for a living, just consult your Guidance System. Dig deep into your feelings and your GS will tell you what feels good and what doesn't. Then pursue what makes you feel good, and you'll be good at it. And somewhere there'll be a market for your skill.

Right behind writing in my life comes investment (playing with money), and I love that too, so naturally I've been successful. In just five years I parlayed $2500 cash into early retirement. That was back in 1964. Mostly for the fun of it, I've also been a hiking guide, primal therapist, forest firefighter, marlin boat crewman, singer, sailor, rattlesnake catcher, river guide, and creative investor. I love to dance, play with babies and puppies, visit with my friends, ponder and write about beliefs, daydream, travel, watch clouds, play basketball and tennis, paint, sculpt, snuggle with my playmate, listen to classical and popular music, and walk in the wilderness.

I rely on the New Way of creating whenever I can figure a way to apply it. And I attribute my success in every area of my life to its deliberate application. It's what makes my life successful and delightful and prosperous and entertaining. I simply listen to my Guidance System and let it point me toward what Feels Good. I make my desires forceful and clear to the Universe, then I put my attention on what feels good, expecting manifestation of my desires. And while I'm waiting—creation isn't usually instantaneous—I simply aim to Feel Good. To avoid the abundant negativity and mass consciousness beliefs that surrounds us, I refuse attention to the dependably negative media (magazines, papers, TV, most movies, the news in all its insidious forms—as well as gloomy and negative people).

Living the New Way has profoundly changed my life by altering my perceptions and judgements of what's important. Gradually, over the years, as I became more adept at attracting and creating, my personal power expanded as my fears diminished, restoring freedom, fun and well-being, bringing me ever increasing success of all kinds. I use my new skills in all kinds of ways, big and small.

For instance, before opening my mail, or picking up the phone, I quickly but forcefully and feelingly "intend and expect" good news. And I've become quite adept at controlling the weather. That may sound impossible, but it's easy. Suppose I've scheduled a hike or international travel, where bad weather could make or break the trip. I'm careful beforehand whenever I think about the trip ahead to visualize the wonderful weather I want, building positive expectation. And I carefully avoid killing my creation by imagining weather I don't want or by consulting weather forecasts. I know—meaning I hold the firm belief—that I can create whatever weather I optimistically expect—as long as I don't counteract my creation with contrary pictures or fears.

Consider a couple of examples. We had planned a week's river rafting trip high in the Brooks Range of Alaska, far north of the Arctic Circle, for early July. Every time I visualized the trip I saw never-ending midnight sun, high season warmth and comfort. To create more of what I wanted, I also saw congenial companions, good fishing and minimal interference from grizzly bears and mosquitos. I visualized a perfect trip, and that's what we got. The guides marveled at conditions. They'd never seen it so warm and free of bugs. It never rained, and more than once we swam in arctic rivers and lakes. Unheard of!

Two months later in September we flew to Italy for a month's hiking high in the southern Alps. Beforehand, I'd imagined perfect, warm, rain-free fall weather. Again, we got exactly what I'd asked for. The veteran guides were amazed. In 40 years they'd never seen a warmer, dryer autumn! At this writing I'm just back from a week in the notoriously wet Olympic National Park in the soggy Pacific Northwest, where we enjoyed rain-free sunshine that defied the odds—all created in advance.

Enough bragging. I hope this picture of how I live and

what I've managed to achieve will help you believe that the New Way might work for you, too. So why not try this no-risk introductory offer in the privacy of your own home for 30 days? If you're not delighted with what you've created—reduced fear, more personal power, growing success and more time spent Feeling Good—you can safely return, at no cost whatsoever, to a life of worry and work!

HOW WILL I DIE?

You've had a taste of how I live. But how will I die...and when? Good questions. Before I knew about the data condensed in this book—especially Chapters 7 & 8—I held the conventional view of death and the hereafter. I expected to get older and more decrepit until finally, after hanging around as long as possible and too sick to go on, I would finally succumb to a grim and fearful death, with little expectation of anything pleasant to look forward to in a possible afterlife. I didn't believe in either heaven or hell, but I vaguely feared a grim purgatory of sorts. When I thought about death the picture was vaguely unpleasant, something increasingly to dread as I grew older.

Now that grim prospect has been magnificently reversed, and I'm free to enjoy the rest of an exciting rewarding life! I actually look forward to the great new adventure of non-physical life in a wonderful hereafter. What a change! Sometimes I can hardly wait to get there—actually envying friends who are dying. Pretty funny! It's supremely comforting to know that I don't have to get sick or decrepit before I die, because I'm in total control of my death, just as I presently control my life. There's really no difference. And be assured that I won't hang around until I can't go on any longer.

At some point the scales will tip in favor of leaving. When I grow weary of this life, a time will come when I'll find more to look forward to on the other side than I do in continuing this lifetime. When that time comes I'll say goodbye to my playmate and all my friends, promising to greet them in grand reunions when they join me in non-physical. Then I'll compose myself for an exciting swift journey to a sweet new life. And I'll peacefully Let Go the way Abraham suggests, slipping easily from this life into the joys of the next. Maybe someday, if I'm lucky, I might even get a chance to join the Abraham Crew!

~

"Nothing can happen more beautiful than death."

–WALT WHITMAN

"Sweet is death who puts an end to pain."

–ALFRED LORD TENNYSON

11

FOUR WHO LET GO

The following four true stories—like Tom's in chapter two—show that anyone can let go of their life force and die when they choose. These people didn't wait around for death to overtake them. They created it. Their stories confirm that all you have to do is make the firm decision to depart this lifetime—and you will. They also reveal that you don't have to be terminally ill, or even old, to successfully let go. You can leave on extremely short notice, with no advance preparation, on your own terms. All it takes is desire, followed by decision.

⤝

Tale Number One was told to me by a hospice staff nurse whose job is looking after the dying, trying to make their last hours as comfortable and contented as possible. Pam, as I'll call her, doesn't usually get well acquainted with her patients. They're often too weak or in pain to give very much, and they're usually not around for very long . But Daniel was a gentle man as well as a gentleman. She told me that, "he wasn't the kind of man you call Dan." He always asked how she felt and showed his appreciation for her every kindness. When she passed his bed, she could always count on a smile, though she knew he was in moderate pain from the stomach cancer that was gradually devouring him. As she did with all her patients, she took time to sit with him and talk when he felt like it. Despite his modest quiet ways, he clearly liked to talk to her.

Over a period of weeks, she came to know quite a bit about him, and about his family. "My survivors," he called them, smiling, or "my heirs." He apparently was wealthy. At least it was apparent that his heirs wanted money. That didn't bother him at all. In fact he joked about it. "Where I'm going, they won't take a check," he liked to say, smiling, "so I may as well give the survivors my money." It was typical of his shy jokes.

Though he was philosophical about leaving his money to his relatives, he didn't enjoy their visits—for good reason. To Pam, his family seemed singularly insensitive, showing no sign of caring about him, taking advantage of his gentlemanly, uncomplaining nature. Helga, his wife, was a large, loud woman who knew what was right in all circumstances and ordered the hospice staff around whenever she appeared. Daniel's sister, Annie, was passive-aggressive, seeming to be as weak as Helga was strong. She whined and complained about her own ailments but never failed to let him know that she needed money.

By comparison, Daniel's son Art was almost refreshingly blunt. All he talked about was money, and there was always a sad story about his bad luck. His various investment schemes always seemed to fail, but clearly he had no interest in getting a job. Art's sister Martha had a rare liver ailment and spoke gibberish when she forgot to take her medicine. She didn't exactly ask for money but you knew she wanted some. Daniel usually asked her if she "needed anything" to find out how much, and to shorten the visit.

Fortunately these people came to visit him one at a time. They didn't seem to like or trust one another. Daniel smiled a good deal during these visits, usually giving them money as soon as possible—and conveniently fell asleep if they stayed too long. Pam found him drained and weakened after every visit. She had talked privately with each of them, explaining that they musn't wear him out, but they didn't seem to understand her. Helga scolded her for babying her husband and worrying too much. "He needs the stimulation," she insisted. "This place is like a tomb, a regular death house. It will kill him if he doesn't get contact with the healthy outside world!"

For several weeks Daniel seemed about the same, but after back-to-back visits by Helga and Martha he seemed to go into a decline. As he grew weaker he slept more and more. His doctor told Pam that he was sinking and probably had only a couple of weeks to live. She felt sorry for

Daniel and wished he would let go and die.

When Helga, who frequently interrogated Daniel's doctor, found out he had only a few weeks to live, she began to appear more often, determined to cheer him up. She also began to organize a deathbed family reunion to say goodbye. "When the father is dying, the family must gather round," she told Pam. "It's important that he isn't alone. The family belongs at the deathbed. I'll bring the priest, too."

The reunion/goodbye gathering was scheduled for ten o'clock on Sunday morning. Art, Martha, and Annie would be there, along with Helga, the priest, and all the other relatives that Helga could round up. On Saturday night, Pam talked quietly with Daniel. When she asked how he felt, he told her he was dreading the family gathering. She nodded, wishing she knew how to help him let go. She says she hinted that he didn't have to be there and tried to give him permission to depart in much the same way that I tried to help Tom in chapter two. When she got up to go, Daniel squeezed her hand and thanked her. She could see the moisture in his half-closed eyes.

Afterward, she went home to bed. Just before dawn she suddenly awoke with a start, alarmed and thinking of Daniel. She immediately got dressed and went down to the hospice. In the predawn light she found him lying on his back, his hands folded across his chest—which was odd because he usually slept curled on his side. She checked his pulse, although she already knew he was gone. He was beginning to cool, but on his face was a look of serene contentment—maybe even the hint of a smile.

❧

Ed was a good and generous friend of mine thirty years ago. He was probably about forty when I met him, a genuine outdoorsman. He owned a little boatyard in the industrial area by the railroad tracks in the city where I lived. He had molds for making fiberglass boats and a fiberglass gun that shot the glass into molds. Peel off the molds, put together the pieces and you had yourself a boat. There were kayaks, canoes, rowboats, sailboats, skiffs and motorboats, all waiting to be built. For me it was boat heaven. I was a young freelance writer, struggling to pay the rent, but I dearly loved small boats. After finishing my day's writing, I would treat myself to a couple of hours with Ed in his boatyard, sanding on whatever boat I happened to be making, talking about boats and fly fishing for trout, two of my favorite subjects. They were Ed's favorites, too, and sometimes we went fishing together.

Ed was a shy, modest man, but he loved to talk about his twin passions, and I never heard him brag. He would rather talk than work, and he often stopped what he was doing to come sit near me on a box to talk laconically about his latest trout fishing trip, interrupting himself occasionally to tactfully show me a better way of doing what I was trying to do. He never seemed to be in a hurry and always had plenty of time to talk. Sometimes when I came in I would find that someone had worked on my boat while I was gone. When I thanked him he seemed embarrassed and changed the subject.

Over the years, I built a lot of boats, taking them to the cabin I owned on a mountain lake, trying them out, then selling the ones I didn't need. At one time I needed nine boats. I knew that Ed was married, but he never talked about his wife. They had no children, just lots of dogs and cats. He lived on the edge of the city and loved to walk in the nearby fields. He loved animals—any kind at all. He modestly told me stories of the wild animals he had tamed. Raccoons, possums, even skunks were welcome to come in his back door and share the food he put out for his dogs and cats. He was proud that the skunks never sprayed, even when he played with them.

Down in the boatyard we had a wood-fired smoker, hidden from snooping industrial inspectors in a corner behind a mold. When either of us came back from a fishing trip with extra trout, we fired it up and smoked them into trout jerky. The fragrance of smouldering hardwood and smoking trout was wonderful. Half a dozen other people dropped in from time to time to work on boats, too, but none of them were fly fisherman. Ed always tried to give them smoked trout. I got casually acquainted with a few of them. Ed seemed to be as helpful and generous to them as he was to me. He didn't like to talk about money. He only charged us—by the pound—for the fiberglass we used. We were supposed to shoot our own glass, but he generally did the hard parts for us without our having to ask. He never asked us to pay anything for rent, utilities his labor, sandpaper, or the use of his molds and tools. When I asked about paying, he said, "Forget it. We'll let the rich customers pay." He knew I didn't have any money.

Then his wife got sick and his demeanor changed. He was quiet and remote, no longer coming over to talk, working away silently on his boats. It was obvious that he was worried. And for good reason. His wife, who I had met only once, soon died of cancer. She had just turned fifty. He was only two years older. After that the boatyard was often padlocked. I learned to call before I came down. When it was open I usually found Ed glum, slouched on a box, unable to rouse his old enthusiasm. I tried hard to interest him in his past pursuits, but it wasn't any use. The light was gone from his life.

Then one Saturday night I was shocked to find him at the door of my apartment. He was carrying a bottle of wine and had obviously been drinking. I invited him in and he insisted on our drinking up his wine. He tried heroically to bring back the old fun, telling familiar stories, recalling boats we had worked on, trout we had caught, our mutual friends, the fishing trips we had taken together. It was painful to see him trying so hard. He must have been as embarrassed as I was. When he got up to leave he told me how much fun he had had, and that we'd have to do it again soon. When he was gone I felt terrible, wishing I could help him but knowing no one could fix his broken heart.

A week later Ed died in his sleep "of natural causes"

according to the newspaper, a healthy man of only 52. He had lasted less than four months after the death of his wife. He had brightened a difficult time in my life, and I missed him for a long time. Now I understand better what must have happened. I don't mourn him anymore because I know he got exactly what he wanted—relief from his pain and a prompt reunion with his wife.

A close friend named Marie told me this sad but revealing story about her grandmother, Rachel. It happened almost fifty years ago, when the culture was more constrained and women's options were fewer. Rachel was a strong and upright, even stiff-backed woman of intelligence, highly educated for her time and strongly matriarchal, with an often hidden kindness and consideration for others. She could be harsh as well as kind, especially when she felt her control was challenged. No one crossed her. She was the heart of a large French family, managing the lives of one and all as needed, but she was well beloved and everyone came to her for her sage advice.

Her only known wrongful deed, confessed to Marie late in life, took place when she was 10, visiting with her mother in a friend's Victorian home. Alone in the parlor, she chanced to see a dainty hand carved from wax in a glass-fronted display case. The wax fingers beckoned irresistibly. An overpowering yearning to chew them seized control of her and she opened the case, took out the hand and bit off the fingers. It was a joy to chew the wax, but unfortunately it soon expanded to fill up her mouth. She grew alarmed and looked frantically for a way to dispose of the growing ball. Finally she hid it beneath the soil in a nearby potted palm. But she felt guilty and guarded her shameful story for half a century.

Over the years, Rachel lived a rigorous healthy life, faithfully serving and looking after her husband Harold and their family, and was proud to say she'd "never been sick a day in my life." Though she had little use for humor, she liked to darkly joke that, "Seymour is going to get me one of these days." Seymour was the proprietor of the funeral parlor on the corner, as well as one of her friends. At the age of sixty, Rachel was still vigorous and firmly in charge of her large extended family.

Then one day she took to her bed and refused to get up. Her family was shocked, but she only deigned to tell them that she needed some rest and time to think. She was clearly upset if not ill. And no one dared to question her. After two days in bed, speaking to no one, she began to summon various members of her family, one by one, to come talk to her. She sat propped like a queen in her four poster, surrounded by lace pillows, her presence and power undiminished though she talked in a whisper. Holding court, she seemed anything but ill, but she refused to talk about her health. Marie still remembers the wise and pragmatic but succinct advice that she and her new husband received in their brief audience, a recipe for health and success—if not happiness.

It sounded very much like deathbed last words, but she didn't pay much attention at the time because she expected Grandma Rachel to be back on her feet within days. So did her doctor, who couldn't find anything wrong with her. But Rachel never left her bed and was dead two days later. She was found one morning by her adoring nurse, a severe but dignified expression on her face. After examining her, the doctor looked perplexed. She had died in her sleep, but he could find no medical reason for her death.

It was years before Marie learned from her mother what had happened.

Rachel had gone to bed after being given positive proof that husband Harold was a child molester. Her best friend and next door neighbor, Marion, a pillar of the community, had convinced Rachel that Harold, had sexually molested her ten-year-old daughter, Debbie. Deep down Rachel had to know about Harold's lecherous behavior toward young girls, but she had carefully avoided knowing the specifics, refusing to accept prior evidence even when it came from her own granddaughter. She'd remained in denial as long as she could. In those days, she hadn't many options. She had no power or money of her own.

Confronted now by unmistakable proof, denial was no longer possible. She must have felt utterly helpless to take action, but living on must have seemed equally intolerable. With no way out, she took to her bed. When her affairs were in order she went to sleep one night expecting not to wake up, and promptly, peacefully died in her bed.

Marie also tells the story of her neighbor, John, the resident water witch on the Puget Sound island where both of them lived. John had come to the island alone as a boy of 17 and gotten a job in a gas station. He was big and athletic with a kind face and a gentle manner. He loved to hunt and fish and roam the island. As the years passed he came to own the gas station, but most of his time was spent working for the water company, locating water wells, always happy to be outdoors. He married a girl named Jane but they had no children. One day when he was seventy, while strenuously helping a friend harvest apples, he suffered a massive heart attack and was rushed by helicopter to the emergency room of a mainland hospital.

He died on the operating table before his heart could be repaired, but after being clinically declared dead, he shocked the medical staff by coming back to life. This Near Death Experience completely changed his life. His former fear off death was utterly gone, and he discovered he possessed intuitive psychic powers. He had always liked people and they found him sensitive to their feelings and problems. Now he found he had a gift for comforting others and helping them face death. Though still working part-time for the water company, he wandered the island, telling the story of his NDE to people he could tell were afraid.

As Marie remembers the story, John was lying on the operating table in terrible pain when suddenly he rose into the sky, his pain vanished, and he found himself peacefully lying on his back on a flat rock high on a hill beneath a wide blue sky. Suddenly a blinding but gentle light was shining down on him, embracing him. He felt a tremendous love pouring into him. Warm energy from the light enveloped him, inviting him to walk into it forever. He could enter the light or go back to his life on the island. He decided he wasn't through living. The doctors were amazed when he opened his eyes and smiled. They couldn't believe he'd survived, but in time he healed completely.

After that his new intuitive powers told him exactly when and where to fish for salmon and hunt deer. Mental instructions led him to often unlikely locations, but the fish or game were always there within minutes. He could have opened a butcher shop, but he never killed more than he and his wife needed. His new found powers also led him to people who were soon going to die. Just by looking at a person he could tell how long they had to live. As a water witch, he knew precisely where his neighbors should drill their wells to be assured of pure, abundant water. And he loved to share his new knowledge with his many friends and acquaintances.

He loved to tell the story of his near death experience, because he wanted to share his discovery that there was nothing at all to fear from death. He made a specialty of counseling the dying in the region, helping them face their coming transitions with fortitude, ease and composure. Marie and her husband went to John when they needed a new well. John offered instead to teach them to water witch so they could find their own water. He came to their property and showed them how to bend a couple of wire coat hangers into witching rods. After showing them how to use them, he took them to a place where water pipes were buried so they could feel the strange pull of the water.

While helping them find a wellsite on their land, he asked them if they believed in Near Death Experiences. But before they could answer he launched into his story. Though Marie's husband was a confirmed skeptic, by the time John was through he was vigorously nodding agreement. Marie says it was impossible to doubt him.

A few years later, when his wife became ill, John focused all his considerable talents on bringing her peace and comfort in her final days. He was able to free her from her fear of death by eloquently describing how wonderful it was to suddenly be free of all pain, and how soothing the gentle light had felt. Once she was gone, he had no reason to live. Though still hale and hearty at 82, John then lay down in his bed and peacefully went to join her. The islanders loved him for his generous gifts, and a reservoir there still bears his name.

⤴

My hope is that this book might carry on John's work, helping readers let go of their groundless fears of death, helping them take control of their own peaceful dignified passing.

~ ~ ~

SOURCES

ABRAHAM

By far the best source of the belief system from beyond, which I call the U-View and the New Way, is the large and growing body of testimony from Abraham, channeled by Esther Hicks. The best way to begin sampling it—direct from the source—is to order AB-1, the *Free Introduction to Abraham* cassette audio tape. Just send $5.00 for S&H, payable to "J&E Hicks," to:

Abraham-Hicks Publications
PO Box 690070, San Antonio TX 78269

Phone: (830) 755-2299 • Fax (830) 755-4179
Website: www.abraham-hicks.com

You might also request the latest Quarterly Journal, "The Science of Deliberate Creation," which provides the schedule of upcoming Abraham weekend workshops around the country, a listing of recent workshop tapes, Abraham books, transcriptions, website address and a tape catalog. Each journal also contains a typical written sample from a recent tape of Abraham answering workshop questions.

Learning to apply the U-View and the New Way is a totally individual quest for the power to deliberately create—with the mind and emotions, not actions—the freedom, joy and growth that are the broad goals of mankind. Abraham is a lively, plain-speaking teacher and advisor, not a guru to be worshiped.

AVATAR

Avatar is utterly different. It doesn't involve channeling and offers no distinct belief system, but it's compatible with Abraham's teachings in terms of how we create, and in its intent to help the individual take back control of his or her life. It agrees that beliefs are everything, expands your awareness to discover your own beliefs. Then it supplies neat techniques for "discreating" unwanted beliefs.

Unlike slow, gentle, inexpensive, independent Abraham study, Avatar is a 6-8 day intensive self-development course costing $2000 that is closely conducted by an Avatar Master, probably in his or her home. It's available worldwide. This blitz approach works well for people with self-esteem or identity problems, those out of touch with their feelings or desiring a fresh start. Like Abraham, it teaches deliberate conscious creation, but because it's confidential there are no materials to take with you for continued study.To investigate Avatar's offerings, contact:

Star's Edge
237 Westmonte Dr., Alamonte Springs FL 32714.

Phones: (407) 788-3090 and 1 (800) 589-3767
Fax: (407) 788-1052

Ask for a free subscription to the Avatar Journal and/ or a phone call from an Avatar Master, or buy the introductory book Living Deliberately by Avatar founder, Harry Palmer, for $15.

BOOKS ON DEATH, DYING AND NDEs

As I've probably made clear, I haven't high regard for most of the vast literature of death. Not only is it resolutely grave and grim, it's based on false assumptions represented as fact that (1) death is always tragic and deplorable—unless, of course, the deceased was bad! (2) death is the end of everything and the beginning of the unknown, (3) fear of death is inescapable, (4) death must be mourned and grieved. (5) The afterlife, being some version of hell, is to be dreaded. But there are exceptions, and the following books were helpful.

BIBLIOGRAPHY

Blackman, Sushila. *Graceful Exits, How Great Beings Die.* Weatherhill: New York, 1997.

Chopra, Deepak. *Quantum Healing.* Bantam New Age: New York, 1989.

Doore, Gary, ed. *What Survives?* Tarcher: Los Angeles, 1990.

Goldberg, Bruce. *Peaceful Transitions.* Llowellyn Publications: Minnesota, 1997.

Humphry, Derek. *Final Exit.* Dell: New York, 1991.

Levine, Stephen. *Who Dies?* Doubleday: New York, 1982.

Kapleau, Phillip. *The Wheel of Life and Death.* Doubleday: New York, 1989.

Kautz, William H. & Branon, Melanie (intro: Kenneth Ryerson). *Channeling: The Intuitive Connection.* Harper & Row: New York, 1973.

Orr, Leonard. *Breaking the Death Habit: The Science of Everlasting Life.* Frog, Ltd., California, 1998.

Palmer, Gregg. *The Trip of a Lifetime.* Harper: San Francisco, 1993.

Roberts, Jane (Seth). *The Individual & the Nature of Events.* Prentice-Hall: New Jersey, 1981.

_____. *The Nature of the Psyche.* Prentice-Hall: New Jersey, 1979.

_____. *The Nature of Personal Reality.* Prentice-Hall: New Jersey, 1974.

Ryerson, Kenneth. *Spirit Communication: The Soul's Path.* Bantam: New York, 1989.

Sechrist, Elsie R. *Death Does Not Part Us.* (Cayce) ARE (Association for Research & Enlightenment): Virginia, 1992.

Weinberg, Steven Lee, ed. *Ramtha.* Sovereignty, Inc.: Washington, 1986.

Wood, Robert S. *Have More Fun!* Condor Books: California, 1995.

∼

About the Author

Robert S. Wood received a BS at the University of California in Berkeley, California, where he was born. He retired at age 34 as staff correspondent for LIFE magazine in San Francisco to travel and write. His nine previous books include *Goodbye, Loneliness!*, an account of his passage through Primal Therapy and his training as a therapist; *Homeopathy, Medicine That Works!* and *Have More Fun!*

Today, he enjoys hiking, gardening, tennis and travel writing. He lives with his wife in Sedona, Arizona, and Lake Tahoe, California.